Conveyancing 2003

Conveyancing 2003

Kenneth G C Reid WS
Professor of Property Law in the University of Edinburgh

and

George L Gretton WS
Lord President Reid Professor of Law in the University of Edinburgh

with additional contributions by Alan Barr and
Andrew J M Steven of the University of Edinburgh

LexisNexis™ UK

Members of the LexisNexis Group worldwide

United Kingdom	LexisNexis UK, a Division of Reed Elsevier (UK) Ltd, 4 Hill Street, EDINBURGH EH2 3JZ and Halsbury House, 35 Chancery Lane, LONDON WC2A 1EL
Argentina	LexisNexis Argentina, BUENOS AIRES
Australia	LexisNexis Butterworths, CHATSWOOD, New South Wales
Austria	LexisNexis Verlag ARD Orac GmbH & Co KG, VIENNA
Canada	LexisNexis Butterworths, MARKHAM, Ontario
Chile	LexisNexis Chile Ltda, SANTIAGO DE CHILE
Czech Republic	Nakladatelství Orac sro, PRAGUE
France	Editions du Juris-Classeur SA, PARIS
Germany	LexisNexis Deutschland GmbH, FRANKFURT and MUNSTER
Hong Kong	LexisNexis Butterworths, HONG KONG
Hungary	HVG-Orac, BUDAPEST
India	LexisNexis Butterworths, NEW DELHI
Ireland	LexisNexis, DUBLIN
Italy	Giuffrè Editore, MILAN
Malaysia	Malayan Law Journal Sdn Bhd, KUALA LUMPUR
New Zealand	LexisNexis Butterworths, WELLINGTON
Poland	Wydawnictwo Prawnicze LexisNexis, WARSAW
Singapore	LexisNexis Butterworths, SINGAPORE
South Africa	LexisNexis Butterworths, Durban
Switzerland	Stämpfli Verlag AG, BERNE
USA	LexisNexis, DAYTON, Ohio

A CIP Catalogue record for this book is available from the British Library.

ISBN 0 406 97366 0

Typeset by Phoenix Photosetting, Chatham, Kent
Printed and bound in Great Britain by Hobbs The Printers Ltd, Totton, Hampshire

Visit LexisNexis UK at www.lexisnexis.co.uk

Preface

This is the fifth annual survey of new developments in the law of conveyancing. As in previous years, it is divided into five parts. There is, first, a brief description of all cases reported since *Conveyancing 2002*, as well as a number of unreported cases. The next two parts summarise, respectively, statutory developments during 2003 and other material of interest to conveyancers. The fourth part is a detailed commentary on selected issues arising from the first three parts. Finally, in Part V, there are two tables. The first, a cumulative table of appeals, is designed to facilitate moving from one annual volume to the next. The second is a table of cases digested in earlier volumes but reported, either for the first time or in an additional series, in 2003. This is for convenience of future reference.

We do not seek to cover agricultural holdings, crofting, public sector tenancies (except the right-to-buy legislation), compulsory purchase or planning law, although this year something is said about new legislation affecting agricultural holdings and crofting. Otherwise our coverage is intended to be complete.

We are grateful to Professor Roddy Paisley of the University of Aberdeen for providing us with the pleadings and opinions in a number of cases from the sheriff court and the Lands Tribunal. Mr Lyall Moodie kindly sent us a decision of the sheriff which we would not otherwise have found. Finally, we are grateful to our colleagues Mr Alan Barr and Dr Andrew Steven for the section on the Land Reform (Scotland) Act 2003, and to Mr Barr for the section on stamp duty land tax.

Kenneth G C Reid
George L Gretton
22 February 2004

Contents

Part I: Cases

Part II: Statutory developments

Part III: Other material

Part IV: Commentary

Part V: Tables

Table of statutes

Table of orders, rules and regulations

Table of cases

Part I

Part I: Cases

The full text of all decisions of the Court of Session is available on the Scottish Courts website: www.scotcourts.gov.uk.

Missives

(1) *Williams v Mutter*
2002 SCLR 1127, Sh Ct

In terms of missives, defects in the central heating system required to be notified within seven days. **Held** that on a proper reading of the clause in question, the notification need not specify all the defects but might be couched in general terms. See **Commentary** p 53.

(2) *Miller Group Ltd v Park's of Hamilton (Holdings) Ltd*
2003 GWD 8-225, OH

Missives were subject to a suspensive condition tied to the obtaining of planning permission. A timetable for the planning application was provided. When the purchasers fell behind, the sellers sought to rescind. **Held:** That, in the absence of contrary stipulation, time was not of the essence. Hence the purchasers must be given a reasonable additional time. See **Commentary** p 51.

(3) *Campbell v Ferguson, MacSween & Stewart*
2003 GWD 14-463, OH

In terms of missives six months were allowed after 'the date of conclusion of missives' for either the purification of suspensive conditions or their waiver by the purchasers. If neither occurred the sellers could resile. The sellers did so. The case turned on the meaning to be given, in the context of a complex contractual history, to 'the date of conclusion of missives'. See **Commentary** p 52.
[Another aspect of this decision is digested at (45).]

(4) *Bluestone Estates Ltd v Fitness First Clubs Ltd*
2003 GWD 27-768, Sh Ct

Another case involving a suspensive condition for planning permission. There was an overriding clause allowing either party to resile if permission had not been obtained by a certain date. It was not obtained, but the purchasers delayed four months before resiling, by which time planning permission was in place. The sellers pled personal bar. **Held:** Despite the delay, the purchasers were entitled to resile. See **Commentary** p 53.

(5) *Smith v Jack*
2003 GWD 5-122, Sh Ct

Technical argument on written pleadings in an action for damages by the sellers following the breakdown of a contract. Proof before answer allowed.

(6) *Glasgow City Council v Caststop Ltd*
2003 SLT 526, IH

Clawback. Missives provided for the payment of additional sums 'in the event that the purchaser achieves planning permission for the erection or redevelopment of the subjects for more than forty-nine residential units'. The planning permission originally granted was indeed for 49 units, but three months later the planning permission was varied to allow 61 units. The second application, however, was not by the purchaser but by its newly-formed wholly-owned subsidiary. Later some of the land was transferred to the subsidiary. When the seller invoked the clawback, the purchaser argued that planning permission had been 'achieved' not by it but by its subsidiary. The clause in the missives did not merely require that planning permission be granted: it required that it be achieved by the purchaser, and it had not been so achieved. **Held:** The clause did not require that the application be made by the purchaser. Rather it had to 'achieve' permission. If the application had been by some remote third party, no credit for the achievement could be given to the purchaser. But here there was direct involvement at least to the extent that the purchaser had formed the subsidiary and procured that it made the relevant application. Hence it could be said to have 'achieved' planning permission for 61 units. The additional sums were accordingly due.

This affirms the decision of the Lord Ordinary reported at 2002 SLT 47 (*Conveyancing 2001* Case (6)).

(7) *Duff v Merrick Homes Ltd*
2003 GWD 11-306, OH

In an earlier litigation the present pursuer had been ordered to implement missives of sale concluded with the present defender. (See *Merrick Homes Ltd v Duff* 1996 SLT 932 and *Merrick Homes Ltd v Duff (No 2)* 1997 SLT 53.) As a result, it appears that the property in question was conveyed to the defender and thereafter sold on. In this present action the pursuer, a party litigant, sought inter alia reduction of the earlier missives (though not of the two subsequent dispositions) and also of the earlier decree. The basis of his action was not clear but there were averments of corruption, blackmail, fraud practised on the court, and corrupt administration of the pursuer's estate during his earlier bankruptcy. The action was dismissed. The pleadings were 'generally incomprehensible' and 'irrelevant and wholly lacking in specification'.

(8) *Scottish Youth Theatre (Property) Ltd v*
RSAMD Endowment Trust Trustees
2003 GWD 27-758, IH

The contract contained an express, though limited, duty of good faith:

> The parties hereby agree that with effect from the date of this agreement the parties shall co-operate with one another in fairness and in good faith on all practical matters of mutual responsibility and interest affecting the implementation of the SYT [pursuers'] Project and the Trust [defenders'] Project respectively and will respond promptly to requests properly made by the other party for approvals, information or assistance.

The SYT Project was for the pursuers to acquire part of a site from the defenders and to build a complex which included rehearsal space. When the pursuers actively pursued the acquisition of a different site for the rehearsal space, the defenders intimated that they regarded the contract as repudiated, and declined to convey the site. **Held:** That, while the pursuers' conduct was disappointing to the defenders, it did not (or not yet) amount to repudiation, in that there had been no default, even by anticipation, in any obligation. In particular, the obligation to build rehearsal space was qualified in certain respects including the availability of adequate funding.

This affirms the decision of the Lord Ordinary reported at *Scottish Youth Theatre (Property) Ltd v Anderson* 2002 SCLR 945 and digested as *Conveyancing 2002* Case (3).

(9) *Smith v Stuart*
2004 SLT (Sh Ct) 2

This is the third recent case to turn on the difficult issue of whether a particular obligation is an 'obligation relating to land' within the Prescription and Limitation (Scotland) Act 1973, Sch 1, para 2(e) and so exempt from the 5-year negative prescription. (The others are *Glasgow City Council v Morrison Developments Ltd* 2003 SLT 263 (*Conveyancing 2002* Case (37)), and *Crabb v Bett Properties Ltd* 2003 GWD 12-357 (Case (15), below).) Obligations exempt from the 5-year prescription prescribe only after 20 years, under s 7 of the 1973 Act.

The facts of this case were unusual. In 1995 the defender undertook in writing:

> I . . . hereby confirm that I will enter into a formal Minute of Agreement with my sister [designed] to the following effect: (1) In the event of the sale of [certain identified land] for agricultural or development purposes half of the sale proceeds will fall to be paid to my sister . . . .

The remaining clauses provided further detail. More than five years passed, and the Minute of Agreement was not entered into. The sister sued to compel performance. The brother pled that his obligation had prescribed. The pursuer argued it was an obligation relating to land. **Held:** That the obligation merely dealt with an agreement to pay money after property had been sold. The sister would not be a party to the sale. The Minute of Agreement itself 'would not have created rights or interests in land or transferred existing rights or interests in land' (para [23]).

We offer three comments. The first is that it is difficult to see why the parties thought that a second document was necessary: it seems that agreement had already been reached in 1995. The second is that normally one cannot 'contract to contract'. (See William W McBryde *Law of Contract in Scotland* (2nd edn, 2001) para 5-13.) That principle is not an unqualified one, but arguably it was relevant here. The third comment is that if the 1995 deed had been an obligation to pay, not an obligation to enter an agreement, then prescription would not have operated. The reason is that prescription starts to run when an obligation becomes prestable, and the obligation to pay would have become prestable only as and when the sale eventually happened.

(10) *Small v Fleming*
2003 SCLR 647, OH

Hillwood Farm, Ratho, near Edinburgh was owned by Tarmac Ltd. Tarmac decided to sell. The pursuer made an offer for £444,444.44. The defender then made an offer for £475,000 (apparently on behalf of another party, the Brewster brothers). The pursuer claimed that he and the defender had entered into a contract to buy and develop the property together, and that his offer was really on behalf of them both, and that the defender was in breach of this contract. After proof absolvitor was granted.

The pursuer led evidence of meetings at which he and the defender allegedly entered into a joint venture for the purchase and development of the property. The defender claimed that matters had never gone beyond the stage of negotiation. There was nothing in writing, or at least nothing in writing by the defender. The pursuer's offer was in his own name. Its terms were not agreed with the defender before it was submitted, nor was a copy of it sent to the defender. Many of the terms of the alleged joint venture agreement were undecided. Even the price seems to have been unsettled, for whilst a figure of £350,000 had been discussed, the pursuer's offer was £444,444.44. He said this was because he had a 'carte blanche mandate' to decide what sum to offer, an assertion that the Lord Ordinary (Lord Macfadyen) found 'quite incredible'. Given these, and other, circumstances, it is perhaps not surprising that it was held that no contract existed.

In the course of his careful opinion, the Lord Ordinary says that 'it is not disputed that joint venture is a species of partnership'. Whilst that may have been a matter of concession, we would with respect suggest that the position is rather more complicated. A joint venture can indeed be a form of partnership. As such it is governed by the Partnership Act 1890. But the primary meaning of the term is a business meaning, and its business meaning can be translated into the conceptions of the law in three different ways, all common in practice. One is the joint venture partnership already mentioned. The second is the joint venture contract, where the joint venturers co-operate without entering into a partnership: contracts of this sort will normally have an express clause stating that there is no intention to enter into a partnership. The third is the joint venture company, in which the joint venturers set up a company, of which they are the shareholders. In practice they will a enter into a shareholders' agreement. To the business person these three forms are much of a muchness, but to the lawyer they are very different. It is less than clear which form of joint venture the pursuer claimed was in contemplation: the negotiations that took place contain pointers to all three. This fact itself may be an additional indication that no consensus between the parties was ever arrived at.

NHBC agreements

(11) *Hughes v Barratt Urban Construction (Scotland) Ltd*
2002 GWD 12-353, 2003 GWD 13-452, OH

The pursuer bought a new flat from Barratt in 1982. More than ten years later, he noticed cracks in the front wall which were eventually found to have been caused by Barratt's failure properly to compact infill on the site. Barratt admitted negligence but argued: (1) on a proper interpretation of the NHBC agreement, any liability thereunder had ceased; and (2) that, since the pursuer could with reasonable diligence have discovered the defect in 1994 but had not raised this action until 2000, he had failed to comply with the five-year period allowed by s 11(3) of the Prescription and Limitation (Scotland) Act 1973. Hence the claim had prescribed.

As to (1) the relevant clause, clause 3, provided that

> The vendor warrants to the purchaser that the dwelling has been or will be built in an efficient and workmanlike manner and of proper materials and so as to be fit for habitation.

But this was qualified by clause 5:

> The vendor shall not be liable to the purchaser in respect of any breach of the warranty set out in Clause 3 if the defect or damage caused by that breach does not first appear until after the expiry of the Initial Guarantee Period unless and until the purchaser has made a claim against the [NHB] Council under Section III of the Insurance Policy in respect of that defect or damage and the Council has disclaimed liability in respect of that claim or any part of it . . . .

The 'Initial Guarantee Period' was two years and had long since expired. Further, the NHBC Insurance Policy had itself expired after ten years, making a claim of the kind contemplated by clause 5 pointless, and indeed no claim had been made. Barratt's argument was that its liability subsisted only for the initial two-year period before passing to the NHBC for the next eight. Thereafter neither was liable. This argument was rejected by the court. Barratt's liability, even after ten years, was affirmed.

As to (2), it was held that the pursuer could not have become aware of the defect until 1995 and so the claim had not prescribed. Damages were awarded, based on the difference, at 1994 prices, between the house's value with the defect and its value without.

Letters of obligation

(12) *Cheval Property Finance plc v Hill*
2003 GWD 36-999, OH

Action by lenders to enforce a letter of obligation. This was a re-financing trans-action in which the debtor became bankrupt. Hence the search was not clear. The defender (solicitor) sought to avoid liability by arguing that (1) the letter of obligation was, necessarily, tied to the loan agreement itself; (2) that agreement provided for a further loan which had never been made; and (3) since the lender was thus itself in breach of contract, it could not enforce the letter of obligation. Unsurprisingly, this argument was rejected by Lord Johnston (para [17]): 'In my opinion the letters of obligation are a free-standing obligation entered into by a third-party, namely the defender, in his capacity as solicitor for the borrower ... While it is possible to draft such letters of obligation as to make them dependent upon the transaction to which they relate, if there was to be any such connection in law it must be, in my opinion, specifically stated and cannot be implied.'

Law of the tenement

(13) *Anderson v Express Investment Co Ltd*
(11 December 2003, unreported), Extra Division

Following a fire in the cavity between two flats, the owner of the lower flat allegedly entered the upper flat (owned by the pursuer) without permission, lifted the floorboards and repaired a fire-damaged load-bearing beam. The pursuer's case was that the repairs had not been properly done; that in time they would have to be re-done; that by the very fact of having been done they deprived the pursuer of the opportunity to have a new beam inserted at the expense of his insurers; and that he had been unable to use the flat pending a proper repair. He sought damages of £100,000. **Held:** That the case as pled did not disclose a proper and consistent claim for damages. It was unclear why the defender's actions, if proved, had caused the loss which the pursuer claimed.

This upholds the decision of the Lord Ordinary reported at 2002 GWD 28-977 (and digested as *Conveyancing 2002* Case (5)).

(14) *Bolam v Glasgow District Council*
2003 Hous LR 15, Sh Ct

This case was decided in 1984 but reported in 2003. A water pipe burst. The water began to seep into the flat below. The occupier contacted the owners of the upper flat, namely the local authority, but it was many hours before a plumber was sent in, and during that time significant damage was caused to the lower flat. It was **held** that in the circumstances the delay was unreasonable and that the defenders were liable for the damage caused.

Boundary walls and gables

(15) *Crabb v Bett Properties Ltd*
2003 GWD 12-375, Sh Ct

Two houses were separated by a mutual gable. When the first house was demolished, the owner surfaced the gable with roughcast rendering. It was averred that the rendering had not been properly applied and in particular that there was a failure to use a bonding agent or metal lath. It was averred that as a result the roughcast and rendering began to spall and break off causing damage to the adjoining house through water penetration. The owner of that house sought (1) £5,000 as damages for the water penetration and (2) an order ordaining the owner of the (former) first house to provide adequate resurfacing. At the time of raising the action more than five years had elapsed since the defect was discovered. Accordingly the defender pled negative prescription. **Held:** Although connected with land, the obligation to pay damages was merely an ordinary obligation to make reparation which had prescribed after five years. The obligation to provide an adequate surface, however, arose *ex dominio* (in fact, by common interest), was thus an obligation relating to land, and hence did not fall within the five-year prescription: Prescription and Limitation (Scotland) Act 1973, Sch 1, para 2(e).

The facts of this case serve to emphasise the continuing obligation on the owner of a mutual gable wall even after the building itself has been demolished. The leading modern case is *Trades House of Glasgow v Ferguson* 1979 SLT 187.

Execution of deeds

(16) *Christie v Bank of Scotland*
2003 GWD 29-803, OH

Pre-1995 law. A wife signed a standard security. Later her husband procured two witnesses to sign who had neither seen her sign nor heard her acknowledge her signature. Hence the deed was void under the old authentication statutes.

Held, following *Boyd v Shaw* 1927 SC 414, that the wife was personally barred from founding on the absence of proper authentication in respect that she had signed the deed and intended it to take effect.

The result would be the same under the Requirements of Writing (Scotland) Act 1995 but for different reasons. By s 2 of that Act an unwitnessed deed is valid, for witnesses are required only for probativity and not for validity. Thus there would be no need to have recourse to personal bar.

[Another aspect of this case is digested at (41).]

Servitudes and rights of way

(17) *Labinski v BP Oil Development Co*
2003 GWD 4-93, IH

The pursuers' predecessors in title granted a servitude for a pipeline to BP. This positive servitude was reinforced by a negative servitude prohibiting building works within ten feet of either side of the pipe. One of the conditions of the servitudes was that

> If at any time the Owner wishes to develop land affected by the pipeline, or to accept an offer from some person who wishes to develop such land, the Owner shall if the said proposed development of the land is prevented in whole or in part by reason only of the existence of the pipeline, give written notice to the Company of the said proposed development including details of the application for and refusal of or conditional grant of planning permission in principle by the Planning Authority. Within six calendar months of the receipt of such written notice, the Company shall give their decision in writing to the Owner that they intend to divert the pipeline or that they intend to pay compensation for all losses arising from their decision not to divert the pipeline, including, without prejudice to the foregoing generality, losses of Development Value.

The pursuer, having been refused planning permission for a development, claimed £31 million from BP. **Held:** Action dismissed. On the pleadings, the existence of the pipeline was not a principal reason for the refusal of planning permission. Instead permission had been refused because the proposed development presented a safety risk; would result in the loss of prime agricultural land; and would be detrimental to the urban form and setting of the nearby town and the appearance of the surrounding countryside. This affirms the decision of the temporary judge, reported at 2002 GWD 1-46 (*Conveyancing 2001* Case (16)).

Doubt is sometimes expressed as to whether a pipeline servitude is one of the servitudes known to the law. In this litigation, however, the validity of the servitude was taken for granted. All doubt will be removed on 28 November 2004 by s 77 of the Title Conditions (Scotland) Act 2003, which is retrospective. However, the common law requirement that a servitude must have a dominant tenement remains, and this can be a difficulty with pipelines.

The defender was the grantee of the servitude. It is open to question whether an obligation to pay compensation would bind its successors in title in the dominant tenement. To bind, a servitude condition would require to be praedial. See D J Cusine and R R M Paisley *Servitudes and Rights of Way* (1998) para 14.08.

(18) *Chilcott v Bedborough*
2003 GWD 18-561, Sh Ct

The pursuers had a servitude of vehicular access over the courtyard next door, owned by the defenders. They sought removal of a fence, with gate, erected by the defenders, on the basis that the defenders were not allowed to interfere with the proper exercise of the servitude. **Held:** Removal would not be granted. The law seeks to strike a balance between the interests of the parties. The pursuers must be allowed to exercise the servitude, but equally the defenders must be allowed to use their property. In the present case the fence had been erected for a legitimate reason (restraint of the defenders' dog), and a gate of sufficient width had been provided which was conveniently close to the pursuers' garage.

(19) *Webster v Chadburn*
2003 GWD 18-562, Sh Ct

Circumstances in which 20 years' use of a private road was **held** not to qualify as possession as of right. Accordingly, no servitude of way was created. See **Commentary** p 65.

(20) *Moncrieffe v Jamieson*
(2003, unreported), Lerwick Sheriff Court

The pursuers had a servitude of vehicular access over a private road leading to their property but, because of a steep fall in the land, it was impossible to drive a vehicle on to their property. **Held:** That the servitude of access included, by implication, a right to park on land immediately adjacent to the road and also belonging to the defender. See **Commentary** p 68.

(21) *David Runciman & Sons v Scottish Borders Council*
2003 SLT 1405, OH

Publicly adopted road, with grass verges flanked by a beech hedge. **Held:** That the verge, and hence the road itself, extended as far as the trunks of the hedge. Accordingly, the roads authority could order the removal of a fence built by the neighbouring landowner on the roadward side of the hedge. See **Commentary** p 70.

(22) *Thomas v Allan*
2004 GWD 1-15, IH

As originally granted, a servitude of way was confined to the track – the usual rule – and did not include the verges. The question was whether this had been altered by a subsequent deed. **Held:** No alteration had taken place. See **Commentary** p 72. This affirms the decision of the sheriff reported at 2002 GWD 12-368 (and digested as *Conveyancing 2002* Case (7)).

Variation and discharge of land obligations

(23) *Kennedy v Campbell*
(LTS/LQ/2003/5) (2 December 2003, unreported), Lands Tribunal

The site at issue was near the centre of Largs, 'a seaside resort attractive to tourists'. The site had views to the sea at the front, and to the hills behind. The applicant planned to demolish the existing villas and build a block of flats – some 18 flats on a one-acre site. Planning permission was being sought but had not yet been granted. The title was subject to a negative servitude, in favour of the immediately adjacent property, prohibiting building beyond the building line. It was this servitude that the applicants sought to have discharged. The application was opposed by the owner of the benefited property and by other affected persons.

Of the three grounds for granting an application under s 1(3) of the Conveyancing and Feudal Reform (Scotland) Act 1970, the Tribunal considered that neither (a) (changes in the land or neighbourhood) nor (b) (burdensome compared with any benefit) had been established. That left (c) (obligation impedes some reasonable use of the land). In order to judge (c), it was necessary to assess the proposed development and its impact. On the evidence, the development would block the view to one side of the benefited property, as well as leading to the garden being overlooked. So far as the wider public were concerned, the development would also be a change for the worse, blocking certain views, and detracting from the attractive openness of this part of Largs. The development had run into substantial public opposition. While, therefore, the development might not be unreasonable in itself, it failed the reasonableness test when viewed from the benefited property or from the perspective of the public at large. The application was therefore refused.

As has been seen, the Tribunal gave weight to the broader concerns of the public. But ordinary neighbours, it emphasised (p 9 of the transcript), had no particular entitlement to protection unless they happened to be benefited proprietors:

> We have no independent role to protect people who are not benefited proprietors. Accordingly, while we can have regard to the impact on these other residents when looking at the question of reasonableness from the public aspect, that is essentially a

matter of public planning control. Proprietors have no inherent legal right to amenity which derives from the restriction on the use which others can make of their own property. We must be careful not to elevate their obvious interest as affected persons into an effective right of control merely because of the high amenity they currently enjoy.

Even as to the wider public interest, the Tribunal's role was limited (at pp 11–12):

We need not, and cannot, put ourselves in the shoes of the planning authority. The real issues relate to matters of private right. We do not require to apply the provisions of the relevant planning legislation. No attempt was made to put before us the terms of the relevant local planning policy. We did not see the relevant Local Plan. In any event, it is not for us to carry out the balancing exercise required of a planning authority. What we have to decide is whether the applicants have established that the proposed development is reasonable from the viewpoint of the public as one factor bearing on overall reasonableness in assessing the proposed use for purposes of ground (c).

Property enquiry certificates

(24) *SPH (Scotland) Ltd v City of Edinburgh Council*
2003 GWD 23-680, OH

The pursuer, a firm of searchers, sought repetition of search fees charged by Edinburgh Council for providing information as to whether any money was owed to the Council by the owners of particular properties (such money potentially leading to the creation of a statutory charge). **Held:** That the Council had failed to show any statutory basis for imposing the charge. Even if it was true, as the Council argued, that it had an overriding duty to secure economy in the use of its resources, this was not information which the Council was bound to provide, and so economy could be secured, if the Council wished, by not providing it.

Registration of title

(25) *Safeway Stores plc v Tesco Stores Ltd*
2003 GWD 20-610, IH

By the Keeper's mistake too much of the *alveus* of a river was included in a registered title. Rectification was sought but was opposed on the basis that the registered proprietor was a proprietor in possession. **Held:** The proprietor was not in possession of the relevant part of the *alveus*, and rectification allowed. See **Commentary** p 91. This affirms the decision of the Lands Tribunal reported at 2001 SLT (Lands Tr) 23 and digested as *Conveyancing 2001* Case (30).

(26) *Griffiths v Keeper of the Registers of Scotland* (20 December 2002, unreported), Lands Tribunal

The holder of a servitude is not a 'proprietor in possession' in relation to the servitude. Accordingly, a servitude can be removed from the Land Register if it can be shown not to have been properly constituted. See **Commentary** p 88.

[Another aspect of this case is digested at (38).]

(27) *Wilson v Inverclyde Council* 2003 SC 366, 2004 SLT 265, IH

This was successor litigation to *Wilson v Keeper of the Registers of Scotland* 2000 SLT 267. (See *Conveyancing 1999* pp 14 and 67). The dispute concerned Greenock Harbour which, since 1987, has been owned by Scottish Enterprise on a title registered in the Land Register. The precise arguments of the pursuers are obscure, but in essence it seemed to be maintained that (1) part or all of the Harbour was formerly owned by the Magistrates of Greenock; (2) the principal conveyance to the Magistrates, in 1772, created a trust; (3) in terms of the trust the property was inalienable; (4) accordingly when the property was eventually conveyed, in 1965, the conveyance was void; (5) the effect of the void conveyance was to make the Register inaccurate by showing Scottish Enterprise (the successor of the 1965 acquirers) as owner; (6) Inverclyde Council was the successor of the Magistrates of Greenock and hence the trustee under the 1772 trust; and (7) the pursuers, as residents of Inverclyde, were beneficiaries under the trust.

The first litigation had sought rectification of the Register. The Register, it was argued, was inaccurate. The 'true' owner was Inverclyde Council, not Scottish Enterprise. Hence the former's name should be substituted for the latter's. That action failed for several reasons. The pursuers failed to establish that the Register was inaccurate. But even if it was inaccurate Scottish Enterprise was proprietor in possession and there were no grounds for seeking rectification. Furthermore, rectification could only be pursued by the trustee under the alleged trust (Inverclyde Council) and not by the beneficiaries.

In this latest action the pursuers sought to meet these difficulties by seeking an order that Inverclyde Council apply for rectification, or lend its name to a rectification action by the pursuers. At first instance the action failed: see 2001 GWD 3-129 (*Conveyancing 2001* Case (29)). The court was not persuaded that the 1772 deed created a trust. Even if it did, beneficiaries could not require a particular course of action of a trustee where this was a matter within the trustees' discretion. And there was nothing in the pleadings to support the idea that rectification would in any event be granted. The present report concerns the appeal to the Inner House, limited, however, to a declarator that the Harbour was held in a trust in respect of which Inverclyde Council was trustee and the pursuers were among the beneficiaries. The appeal failed. The feu contract of 1772 did not, in the court's view, create a trust separate from the ordinary common good of the burgh.

In an apparently related action, the same pursuer was unsuccessful in a claim for damages in respect inter alia of interdict which, Scottish Enterprise conceded, had been wrongly obtained: see *Wilson v Scottish Enterprise* 2003 GWD 13-454.

Right-to-buy legislation

(28) *Queens Cross Housing Association v McAllister*
2003 SC 514, 2003 SLT 971, IH

The right to buy, in its original form, applied not only to local authority landlords but also to registered housing associations. The Housing (Scotland) Act 1988 removed the right to buy from new housing association tenants, but retained it for old ones. Section 43(3) provided that where a pre-1988 tenant took a new tenancy with the same housing association, the existing right to buy would apply to the property which was subject to the new tenancy. This case turned on the exact meaning of s 43(3). It upholds the decision of the Lands Tribunal reported at 2002 SLT (Lands Tr) 13 (and digested as *Conveyancing 2002* Case (26)).

(29) *Johnston v Link Group Ltd*
2003 GWD 29-822, Lands Tribunal

In this right-to-buy case there was a dispute as to the terms of the disposition to be granted. The landlords were **held** entitled to insist on (1) a right to erect scaffolding; (2) an access right; and (3) an obligation on the buyer to contribute to the maintenance of mutual areas. (The buyer was prepared to accept a maintenance obligation but only for a smaller area.) The Tribunal also ruled on the boundary of the area to be disponed.

Leases

(30) *Keenan v Whitehead*
2003 GWD 10-289, Sh Ct

A lease was granted for a three-year period ending on 1 November 2001. On 1 October 2001 the owner wrote to the tenants saying that they would have to accept responsibility for the rates. The tenants removed on 31 March 2002. The landlord sued for rent for the year up to 1 November 2002, arguing that the lease had been tacitly relocated. The sum sued for was inclusive of the rates, which the landlord claimed were now the tenants' responsibility. The Sheriff (D J Cusine) rejected this argument. If the lease had been tacitly relocated then it subsisted on the same terms, and thus the landlord could not argue that responsibility for the rates had shifted. The letter of 1 October could not be taken as a notice to quit, terminating the three-year lease, if only because notice to quit must normally be

40 clear days before the ish. At most the pursuer was entitled only to (1) rent at the old rate up to 31 March 2002 and (2) damages for premature termination of the lease as tacitly relocated. Given the state of the pursuer's pleadings the action was dismissed.

(31) *Oak Mall Greenock Ltd v McDonald's Restaurants Ltd* 2003 GWD 17-540, OH

This was a decision on the enforceability of a keep-open clause in a commercial lease. See **Commentary** p 54.

(32) *Homebase Ltd v Scottish Provident Institution* 2004 SCLR 44, IH

This was a dispute as to the proper construction of a rent review clause. The lease said that the rent was to be reviewed on the basis of unchanged rights of use. The question was whether, on a proper construction, the lease allowed the tenant to use the property for any non-food retailing or, more narrowly, only for DIY and garden-centre retailing. The landlord contended for the broader construction, and the tenant for the narrower one. The arbiter found for the landlord. The tenant appealed by way of stated case. The appeal was successful.

The lease provided that the rent review was to be on the assumption 'that the landlord and the tenant have complied with all the obligations imposed on them respectively under these presents . . . .' One of the obligations was as to use of the premises:

> Not to use or permit the Premises to be used except as a non-food retail warehouse for any use falling within Class 1 of the Schedule to the Town and Country Planning (Use Classes) (Scotland) Order 1989 (with ancillary stores and offices) together with car parking, servicing and landscaping . . . .

That indicates that any non-food retail use would be permissible, and on that basis the arbiter found for the landlord. However, the lease also required the tenant to comply with planning law. There was a s 50 agreement under the Town and Country Planning (Scotland) Act 1972 (in modern terms a s 75 agreement under the Town and Country Planning (Scotland) Act 1997) whereby the range of goods to be retailed would be limited to what was allowed by the local authority. The local authority had, with reference to the s 50 agreement, issued the following letter:

> I hereby confirm that Tayside Regional Council has been consulted as to the range of goods to be retailed from the proposed retail warehouse, ie that range of goods normally retailed in DIY outlets, including garden centre with sales related thereto . . .
> I further confirm that the District Council consents to the sale of range of goods as specified.

The net result was that the tenants were restricted to DIY and garden-centre trading. It followed that the rent review should be on that basis.

(33) *City Wall Properties (Scotland) Ltd v Pearl Assurance plc* 2003 GWD 27-769, OH

This too was a dispute as to the proper construction of a rent review clause. See **Commentary** p 59.

(34) *Howgate Shopping Centre Ltd v Catercraft Services Ltd* 2004 SLT 231, OH

This too was a dispute as to the proper construction of a rent review clause. See **Commentary** p 58.
[Another aspect of this case is digested at (53).]

(35) *Kingston Communications (Hull) plc v Stargas Nominees Ltd* 2003 GWD 33-946, OH

In 1997 Stargas Nominees Ltd granted a 25-year lease of a unit at Edinburgh's Gyle shopping centre to Kingston SCL Ltd ('KSCL') – a company later called Telesens KSCL Ltd and later still T K Realisations Ltd. The tenant's parent company, Kingston Communications (Hull) plc ('Kingston'), guaranteed the rent. The guarantee also provided that if the tenant became insolvent the landlord could require the guarantor to take over the lease – a common provision nowadays. In 2000 Kingston sold KSCL to Telesens AG. In 2002 KSCL went into receivership. The receivers granted what purported to be a licence to a company called Convergys EMEA Ltd to occupy the premises in exchange for payment. Meanwhile the landlord called on Kingston (1) to pay arrears of rent and (2) to take over the lease. Kingston refused and litigation ensued. Kingston argued that the landlord had re-let the premises to Convergys EMEA Ltd and that the lease had thus been repudiated. As a result the guarantee was no longer enforceable. This argument failed and the claims of the landlord were upheld. The occupation by Convergys EMEA Ltd was on the basis of a contractual arrangement with the joint receivers of KSCL and not on the basis of a lease from Stargas Nominees Ltd.

(36) *Allied Dunbar Assurance plc v Superglass Sections Ltd* 2003 GWD 36-1013, OH

This case raised the issue of whether tenants were unable to bring the lease to an end by virtue of a break clause due to the fact that they were themselves, allegedly, in breach of maintenance obligations under the lease. See **Commentary** p 56.

(37) *Hiskett v Wilson*
2003 GWD 38-1040, OH

What happens if there is a lease to a partnership and the partnership is dissolved? Does the lease fall? Does it perhaps depend on what the lease says? Does it perhaps depend on what the partnership deed says? Does it perhaps depend on whether the dissolution is a 'technical' one, with the business continuing under the same firm name and with most of the partners the same, or is a more substantive dissolution required? The area is one of considerable difficulty, partly because of certain obscurities in the law of partnership. Important decisions in this area include *Inland Revenue v Graham's Trustees* 1971 SC (HL) 1, *Jardine-Paterson v Fraser* 1974 SLT 93, *Lujo Properties Ltd v Green* 1997 SLT 225, and *Moray Estates Development Co v Butler* 1999 SLT 1338, 1999 SCLR 447. For some discussion of the issues, see *Conveyancing* 1999 pp 44–8.

In 1961 two neighbouring farms in Kincardineshire, namely Mains of Dellavaird and Milton of Dellavaird, were let to George Wilson and his son George S Wilson. One issue was whether one farm was let to the one and the other to the other or whether there was a single lease of both farms to both men, in common. On this point it was held that the latter was the correct interpretation. Later George Wilson died. There was no transfer of his interest to anyone and there was no new lease. What happened on the ground is that George S Wilson carried on farming both farms and paying the rent. But what happened legally was disputed. Both parties agreed that a new tenancy came into existence, by implication. But who was the tenant? The landlords claimed that it was the firm of G & G Wilson, of which George S Wilson and his wife Marion were the partners. The defenders argued that the tenant was George S Wilson. On this point the Lord Ordinary (Drummond Young) found for the landlords. In 2001 George S Wilson's son, George G Wilson, had been assumed as a partner, and landlords claimed that this dissolved the partnership with the result that the lease was at an end. They sought decree of removing. They were successful.

In 2003 a joint report by the English and Scottish Law Commissions was published on partnership law (Scot Law Com No 192, Law Com No 283, available on www.scotlawcom.gov.uk). If implemented, the Partnership Act 1890 would be repealed and replaced with a wholly new Act. One aspect of the proposals is that in the future a partnership is much more likely to be deemed to continue to exist notwithstanding a change in membership.

(38) *Griffiths v Keeper of the Registers of Scotland*
(20 December 2002, unreported), Lands Tribunal

A 'servitude' was imposed in the assignation of a long lease. **Held:** That this was not valid as a condition or stipulation within s 3(2) of the Registration of Leases (Scotland) Act 1857. See **Commentary** p 60.

[Another aspect of this case is digested at (26).]

Trusts, liferents and tailzies

(39) *Armstrong v G Dunlop & Sons' Judicial Factor*
2003 GWD 31-858, IH

This is the latest round in a long dispute. (See also *Armstrong, Petitioner* 1988 SLT 255, *G Dunlop & Sons' Judicial Factor v Armstrong* 1994 SLT 199, and *G Dunlop & Sons' Judicial Factor v Armstrong* 1995 SLT 645.) Mr and Mrs Dunlop were married and were the partners of a farming partnership, Messrs G Dunlop & Sons. They became estranged about 1982. In 1986 Mr Dunlop petitioned for the dissolution of the partnership and for the appointment of a judicial factor to the partnership assets, and an interlocutor to that effect was pronounced in 1987. Soon afterwards the parties were divorced, and it was agreed that a farmhouse with garden ground should be conveyed to Mrs Dunlop. For reasons that are unclear this never happened, but it seems that Mrs Dunlop did, over the years, live in the property. The judicial factor wished to sell it. In 1994 he obtained an interdict to stop Mrs Dunlop interfering in the sale of the property, but no sale seems ever to have occurred. In 2001 he obtained decree against her for possession. In the present action Mrs Dunlop sought reduction of that decree, interim interdict against its enforcement, and declarator that she was entitled to receive from the judicial factor a disposition of the property. Her reason for reduction was that she had been in ill health and had thus been unable to give proper instructions. The Lord Ordinary granted her interim interdict: see 2004 SLT 155 (digested as *Conveyancing 2002* Case (48)). In this appeal the reclaiming motion was refused. The opinion is brief.

Standard securities and floating charges

(40) *Royal Bank of Scotland plc v Wilson*
2003 SC 544, 2003 SLT 910, 2003 SCLR 716, IH

This case, which is about the doctrine established by *Smith v Bank of Scotland* 1997 SC (HL) 111, affirms the decision of the sheriff reported at 2001 SLT (Sh Ct) 2, and digested as *Conveyancing 2000* Case (53). See **Commentary** p 74.

(41) *Christie v Bank of Scotland*
2003 GWD 29-803, OH

Another case on the doctrine established by *Smith v Bank of Scotland* 1997 SC (HL) 111. See **Commentary** p 77.

[Another aspect of this case is digested at (16).]

(42) *Thomson v Royal Bank of Scotland*
2003 SCLR 964, OH

Another case on the doctrine established by *Smith v Bank of Scotland* 1997 SC (HL) 111. See **Commentary** p 78.

(43) *Unity Trust Bank plc v Frost*
2003 GWD 32-888, OH

This was an action to enforce a standard security granted by Mr and Mrs Frost. Mr Frost, a party litigant, is well known in the courts, and not only in connection with his litigations with Unity Trust Bank, though these have been substantial. (They have already reached the law reports twice: *Frost v Unity Trust Bank plc* 1997 SLT 1358 and *Frost v Unity Trust Bank* plc 2000 SLT 952.)

In this particular case the defences were as follows. (1) That the loan was not from the pursuer but from another bank. This was rejected. (2) That the loan was *ultra vires* of the pursuer. This was rejected. (3) That there was no obligation to repay because the defenders were entitled to 'offset' sums allegedly due to them by the pursuer. (In the words of the Lord Ordinary (Lord Eassie) Mr Frost claimed that 'Unity were due him various sums for valuations and reports on matters relating to possible corporate clients and there were other claims against the pursuers by companies with which he was involved.') This was rejected. (4) That the pursuer was operating outwith the required financial ratios under applicable banking legislation, and therefore was not entitled to ask for repayment of loans that it made. This too was rejected.

Solicitors and estate agents

(44) *Hands v R & J A MacCallum*
2003 GWD 10-294, OH

The pursuer sought damages from his former solicitors for alleged negligence relating to property development. The precise factual basis of the pursuer's case is unclear, but it seems to have centred on an alleged failure to give proper advice as to some aspect of planning law. The alleged negligence happened about 1983, and the present action was raised in 1999. It was **held** that any claim that may have existed had prescribed negatively.

As so often in negligence actions where the defender pleads negative prescription, the pursuer sought to invoke s 11(3) of the Prescription and Limitation (Scotland) Act 1973, which provides that the short negative prescription does not run while 'the creditor was not aware, and could not with reasonable diligence have been aware, that the loss, injury or damage ... had occurred'. But it was held that the pursuer's pleadings did not contain a sufficient basis for this argument.

(45) *Campbell v Ferguson, MacSween & Stewart*
2003 GWD 14-463, OH

Sellers withdrew from missives. The disappointed purchaser raised an action for damages of £1,391,535. The action was against his solicitors, on the ground that they should have prevented the withdrawal by waiving certain suspensive conditions. The pursuer would have to have surmounted a number of hurdles to establish his case, but in the event he failed at the first of these, which involved the question of what, precisely, the missives meant.

[Another aspect of this case is digested at (3).]

(46) *Adams v Thorntons*
2003 GWD 27-771, OH

This was a claim for damages for alleged negligence. The pursuer entered into a complex property transaction for the purchase and redevelopment of property called Airlie Lodge, Broughty Ferry. The transaction went wrong, allegedly because of the negligence of the defenders. The defenders pled (inter alia) negative prescription, since the alleged negligence took place in December 1990, whereas the action was not raised until October 2001. The pursuer responded by invoking s 11(3) of the Prescription and Limitation (Scotland) Act 1973 (see above). A proof before answer took place, as a result of which it was held that any claim that there might have been had indeed prescribed.

A curious feature of the transaction was that the defenders acted for numerous different parties, including (1) the pursuer; (2) the pursuer's business partner; (3) the two sellers of one part of Airlie Lodge (one of whom was a partner of the defenders); (4) the seller of the other part of Airlie Lodge; (5) a company controlled by the pursuer that was also involved in the transaction; (6) a company controlled by the pursuer's business partner that was also involved in the transaction; and (7) the bank that was providing much of the funding. (For an earlier stage of this litigation see *Adams v Thorntons* 2002 SCLR 787, digested as *Conveyancing 2002* Case (57).)

(47) *Lloyd v Campbell Riddell Breeze Paterson*
(A1700/01) (25 March 2003, unreported), Glasgow Sheriff Court

This was another case in which a damages claim for alleged negligence in a conveyancing matter was held to have prescribed negatively. (What the negligence was supposed to have been is less than clear.) The action was raised in April 2001. The defenders had ceased to act for the pursuer in April 1991, and the loss arising from their alleged negligence occurred late in 1992 or early 1993. Presumptively, therefore, any claim had prescribed. The pursuer founded on s 11(3) of the Prescription and Limitation (Scotland) Act 1973 (see above). He also founded on s 6(4), which excludes any period during which the creditor was induced to refrain from suing by false statements by the debtor. It was **held** that the pursuer's averments as to why he had taken so long to sue were unsatisfactory, and accordingly any claim had indeed prescribed.

(48) *George Wimpey UK Ltd v Brown*
2003 SLT 659, HC

Prosecutions under the Property Misdescriptions Act 1991 are very rare. This was one. George Wimpey UK Ltd was prosecuted for having falsely told prospective purchasers of its houses at Avonlea Gate, Hamilton that, in the words of the complaint, 'houses belonging to Scottish Homes at Highstonehall Road situated adjacent to said Avonlea Gate, Hamilton, were to be demolished and that said demolition would occur during 1999'. The company was tried and convicted. It appealed against conviction, successfully. It seems that there was a collection of older buildings at Highstonehall Road and Ewart Crescent and that in the trial these had been treated as a group. It was proved at the trial that the houses at Ewart Crescent had not been demolished, but it seems that the prosecution had not specifically led evidence that the houses at Highstonehall Road had not been demolished, and it was that road only that was specified in the complaint. In the words of the appellate court:

> The sheriff was no doubt right that Highstonehall Road and Ewart Crescent together comprised, for some purposes, a single category of 'older houses'. It does not, however, follow in our opinion that the distinction between Ewart Crescent and Highstonehall Road can be completely elided when it comes to deciding what has been proved as to the falsity of the statements. It is, in our view, clear that the evidence given by Mrs Harvey, which would have supported the libel if it had related to houses in Highstonehall Road, cannot be interpreted as extending beyond its terms. It related to Ewart Crescent. It did not relate to Highstonehall Road. There is therefore, in our opinion, no support in the evidence of Mrs Harvey for the falsity of the statements relating to houses in Highstonehall Road.

Boundary disputes/prescription

(49) *Young v West*
(A128/98) (3 September 2003, unreported), Elgin Sheriff Court

The defender built a commercial car-wash partly on ground belonging to the pursuer. **Held:** That although the pursuer was not personally barred from founding on the encroachment, the court would exercise its discretion not to require the removal of the car-wash. See **Commentary** p 83.

(50) *Canmore Housing Association Ltd v Bairnsfather*
(7 January 2004, unreported), OH

Boundary dispute which only a full proof would resolve. Meanwhile the petitioners sought interdict and an order that the respondents remove vehicles from the strip in dispute. The petition was refused on a number of grounds, including the fact that the status quo favoured the respondent and that, in any event, such plans as were produced suggested that the respondent might have a title to at least part of the strip.

Judicial rectification

(51) *Co-operative Wholesale Society Ltd v Ravenseft Properties Ltd* 2003 SCLR 509, OH

A lease contained two separate keep-open clauses. By minute of variation, one was deleted. Later the tenant sought rectification of the minute of variation to the effect of deleting the second clause also, which had been overlooked. **Held**, after a proof, that the application should be refused. The parties' common intention was to delete one clause only. That intention had been given proper effect by the minute of variation. It did not matter that the intention may have been formed partly in ignorance. See **Commentary** p 102.

This case was also reported at earlier stages: see 2001 GWD 24-905 (*Conveyancing 2001* Case (80) and Commentary p 121), and 2002 SCLR 644 (*Conveyancing 2002* Case (66) and Commentary p 99).

(52) *Jones v Wood* (27 October 2003, unreported), Dumfries Sheriff Court

A farm was sold in two parts. The deed plans were incorrect and, by mistake, conveyed too much land to one disponee and too little to another. When the shortchanged disponee sought rectification of the plan, this was opposed by a successor of the other disponee, pleading s 9 of the Law Reform (Miscellaneous Provisions) (Scotland) Act 1985. **Held**, after a proof, that the circumstances for a s 9 defence had not been made out. See **Commentary** p 104.

(53) *Howgate Shopping Centre Ltd v Catercraft Services Ltd* 2004 SLT 231, OH

This was a dispute as to the proper construction of a rent review clause. Although the landlords succeeded on the construction of the clause, the court also considered the landlords' alternative argument, that the clause in the sublease failed to express the common intention of the parties, and that it should be rectified to make clear that the full market rent was due. There was some discussion as to what was relevant evidence. As the sublease was granted in implement of missives, the court considered, surely correctly, that the only relevant evidence was the missives themselves. They represented the parties' common intention. Hence the landlords' task was to establish that the missives provided for full market rent. (In the court's view this could successfully be done.) Evidence of prior negotiations was irrelevant unless the missives too were challenged as not representing the parties' intentions. No such challenge had been made. As Lord Macfadyen said (at para [50]):

> If the intention had been to go one stage further back, and to rely on a common intention of the parties to the informal agreement which lay behind the missives, it would, in my opinion have been necessary for the pursuer to seek (a) rectification of the missives, and then (b) consequential rectification of the sub-lease.

[Another aspect of this case is digested at (34).]

Matrimonial Homes Act

(54) *Stevenson v Roy*
2003 SC 544, 2003 SCLR 616, IH

Section 6(3) of the Matrimonial Homes (Family Protection) (Scotland) Act 1981 (as amended) provides that occupancy rights prescribe if 'the entitled spouse has permanently ceased to be entitled to occupy the matrimonial home, and at any time thereafter a continuous period of 5 years has elapsed during which the non-entitled spouse has not occupied the matrimonial home'. The question for decision was whether the raising of an action to enforce occupancy rights interrupts the running of prescription (the general rule being that prescription is interrupted by the raising of an action). It was held in the Outer House that it did not (2002 SLT 445, digested as *Conveyancing 2002* Case (67)), and this decision has now been affirmed. As the Division itself observes, the result may be unsatisfactory, since the pursuer's rights, actual or alleged, will suffer from delays outwith her control. The Division suggests that the possibility of legislative reform should be considered. A valuable discussion of the case by Ken Swinton can be found at (2003) 71 *Scottish Law Gazette* 112.

Diligence and insolvency

(55) *Advocate General for Scotland v Taylor*
2003 SLT 1340, IH

The traditional Scottish system of diligence on the dependence has long been criticised as unfair on defenders. Whilst most other legal systems allow broadly equivalent procedures, only in Scotland has the law allowed the pursuer to obtain warrant for diligence on the dependence automatically, as of right. Yet whilst vigorous criticism of our system goes back to the eighteenth century, nothing has been done. It is in such situations that one is grateful to the European Convention on Human Rights.

In *Karl Construction Ltd v Palisade Properties plc* 2002 SC 270, 2002 SLT 312 (*Conveyancing 2002* Case (68)), an inhibition on the dependence was recalled on the ground that it violated the defender's ECHR rights. What was objectionable was not the possibility of diligence on the dependence as such, but rather the too-easy manner in which the pursuer could obtain a warrant. The decision was not appealed, and since then there have been numerous other first-instance cases on the issue, and a considerable degree of uncertainty as to the law. The present case is the first time the matter has been considered by the Inner House. It has to be said that the decision (which, curiously, took about a year to come out) is a little disappointing. It is sketchy, and for solid discussion one must return to Lord Drummond Young's opinion in *Karl*. The Division upheld the view that the system (ie the pre-*Karl* system) is incompatible with the ECHR, and that warrant to inhibit on the dependence (and likewise warrant to arrest on the dependence) must not be granted automatically as part of the summons, but only by way of motion. In other words, the granting of the warrant must be a judicial act. This brings us into line with other European countries.

But that is not all. If the pursuer is not entitled to a warrant as of right, but only by satisfying the court that the warrant should be granted, what must he show? What is the justification for a warrant? In *Karl* (at para [54]) Lord Drummond Young summarised his views thus:

> Four requirements must be satisfied if a right of protective attachment of immovable property during litigation is to conform to Article 1 of the First Protocol [of the ECHR]. These are as follows:
>
> (1) The pursuer must establish a prima facie case on the merits of the action.
>
> (2) The pursuer must establish that there is a specific need for an interim remedy; this will generally involve demonstrating either that there is a significant risk of the defender's insolvency or that the defender is taking steps to conceal or dissipate his assets or that there is a significant risk that the defender will remove his assets from the jurisdiction.
>
> (3) A hearing must take place before a judge at which the last two matters are considered.
>
> (4) If protective attachment is used without an objective justification, and in particular if the pursuer is unsuccessful in the action, the defender should be entitled to damages for any loss that he has suffered in consequence of the attachment.

In *Taylor* counsel for the defender founded on Lord Drummond Young's position, including the second point, namely that the pursuer must show that there exists a specific need for the remedy. But counsel for the pursuers urged that the test should be limited to the prima facie strength of the pursuer's case. The Division agreed (para [34]):

> We have in mind that the applicant for a warrant or for letters of inhibition need only establish a prima facie case on the merits of the action. The necessity for diligence need not be demonstrated although it may no doubt assist the grant if it is. But the applicant will have to demonstrate that the diligence sought is proportionate to the claim.

We would respectfully suggest that the approach of Lord Drummond Young in *Karl* is preferable. Suppose that a local builder does some repairs to a branch of a major Scottish bank. There is a dispute about the bill and in the end the builder decides to sue. He has a prima facie case. Can that justify diligence on the dependence? It seems arguable that a warrant which is granted merely on the basis of a prima facie case is still incompatible with the ECHR.

It is, we would suggest, relevant that there has always been one category of diligence on the dependence where automatic warrant is not granted. This is the case of diligence in security of a future debt. In such cases the pursuer has always had to satisfy the court that 'special circumstances' existed to justify the warrant. See eg Gretton *Law of Inhibition and Adjudication* (2nd edn, 1996). This makes good sense and it would be interesting to know why that test was not thought the appropriate one.

The decision of the court was made on 5 November 2003, and two days later an Act of Sederunt was made: Act of Sederunt (Rules of the Court of Session Amendment No 6) (Diligence on the Dependence) 2003, SSI 2003/537. This came into force on 10 November. In truth, this was the AS that should have been made as soon as *Karl* was decided. It amends the Rules of Court so as to require that warrants for inhibition on the dependence be obtained by motion. However, it says nothing as to the basis on which such a motion can be granted. The AS also impacts slightly on s 155 of the Titles to Land Consolidation (Scotland) Act 1868 under which a notice of inhibition can be registered in the Register of Inhibitions and Adjudications: now what is registered is a notice of the certified copy of the interlocutor granting authority for inhibition.

(56) *Walker v Roberts*
2003 GWD 32-889, OH

This was another case on inhibition on the dependence. Recall was granted on the basis of the *Karl* doctrine.

(57) *Amalgamated Roofing and Building Company v Wilkie*
2003 GWD 40-1071, OH

This was another case on the validity of diligence on the dependence. The pursuers sued the first defender for £76,123. In September 2000 they inhibited on the dependence. In September 2001 the first defender disponed a property to the second defender. The latter granted a standard security to the third defender. (The opinion of Temporary Judge Coutts QC does not disclose whether these deeds were registered, and, if so, in which register.) In October 2001 the pursuers obtained decree. They then raised the present action for reduction *ex capite inhibitionis* of the disposition and the standard security.

The defence was that the inhibition had originally been an inhibition on the dependence, and that it violated the *Karl* principles. Hence it could not be founded on. This defence was rejected, surely rightly. The *Karl* doctrine meant that the first defender could have sought recall. But he did not do so, and even if he had done so he might well have been unsuccessful. Inhibitions on the dependence obtained before *Karl* are not void. At most they may be recallable.

(58) *Henderson v 3052775 Nova Scotia Ltd*
2003 GWD 40-1080, OH

This was an action for the reduction of a disposition as a gratuitous alienation. Letham Grange Development Co Ltd was the owner of Letham Grange Country Club and Resort, Arbroath. Its major shareholders were members of the Liu or Liou family: Shiau Cheng Tzu Liou, Jiah Jow Liou, Dong Guang (or Kuang) Liu, and King Hsia Chou Liu, and these persons seem also to have been major creditors of the company. In February 2001 the company granted a disposition of the property to 3052775 Nova Scotia Ltd for £248,000. At the time Dong Guang Liu was managing director of both the disponer and of the disponee. The opinion mentions that 'the agents' (whether this means the agents for the disponer or the agents for the disponee is unclear) advised at the time that 'if the transfer of Letham Grange is at a figure under its true value then such a transfer could be attacked in the future by any Liquidator of Letham Grange'.

The remark proved prescient. The disponer subsequently went into liquidation, and the liquidator raised an action to reduce the disposition as a gratuitous alienation, the true value of the property having been somewhere in the general region of £2,000,000. The defender pled that in addition to the price it had assumed liability for various debts of the disponer. Evidence for this was, however, inadequate, and summary decree was granted. The fact that stamp duty had been paid on the basis of the figure of £248,000 clearly weighed with the Lord Ordinary (Lord Carloway). The case is a fact-specific one, but it is instructive nevertheless. One odd feature of the case is that the opinion does not say whether the disposition was ever registered.

Part II

Part II: Statutory developments

The text of all Acts and statutory instruments, both of Scotland and of the United Kingdom, is available on www.hmso.gov.uk.

Land Reform (Scotland) Act 2003 (asp 2)

See **Commentary** p 131.

Public Appointments and Public Bodies etc (Scotland) Act 2003 (asp 4)

For the most part this Act has nothing to do with conveyancing. However it includes provisions abolishing the Scottish Conveyancing and Executry Services Board (s 4) and transferring its regulatory powers to the Law Society of Scotland (s 12). Licensed conveyancers ('independent conveyancing practitioners') are given certain powers of notaries public when the need arises in the course of conveyancing services (s 14). The Act is not yet in force.

Building (Scotland) Act 2003 (asp 8)

This Act prospectively repeals and replaces the Building (Scotland) Act 1959. See **Commentary** p 85.

Title Conditions (Scotland) Act 2003 (asp 9)

Following the Abolition of Feudal Tenure etc (Scotland) Act 2000, this is the second part of the Scottish Executive's overhaul of land law. See **Commentary** p 106.

Homelessness etc (Scotland) Act 2003 (asp 10)

This amends in a number of respects the homelessness provisions of the Housing (Scotland) Act 1987. For the conveyancer, the most important change is that heritable creditors must notify local authorities where enforcing a standard security in respect of residential property. See Schedule, para 1 of the Homelessness etc (Scotland) Act 2003, amending the Conveyancing and Feudal Reform (Scotland)

Act 1970. The rule applies to calling up notices, notices of default, and applications under s 24 of the 1970 Act.

Agricultural Holdings (Scotland) Act 2003 (asp 11)

In this series we do not seek to cover agricultural tenancies. However, some mention of this important statute seems appropriate. See **Commentary** p 63.

Salmon and Freshwater Fisheries (Consolidation) (Scotland) Act 2003 (asp 15)

This Act consolidates the legislation relating to salmon and freshwater fisheries, including the Salmon and Freshwater Fisheries (Protection) (Scotland) Act 1951 and the Freshwater and Salmon Fisheries (Scotland) Act 1976. It implements a Report by the Scottish Law Commission on *Consolidation of Certain Enactments Relating to Salmon and Freshwater Fisheries in Scotland* (Scot Law Com No 188, 2002; available on www.scotlawcom.gov.uk).

Finance Act 2003 (c 14)

Part 4 of this Act introduced stamp duty land tax in place of stamp duty, with effect from 1 December 2003. See **Commentary** p 141.

Commencement of the Abolition of Feudal Tenure etc (Scotland) Act 2000 (asp 5)

Part 4 of the 2000 Act, allowing superiors to preserve feudal burdens by registration of a notice, was brought into force on 1 November 2003, by the Abolition of Feudal Tenure etc (Scotland) Act 2000 (Commencement No 1) Order 2003, SSI 2003/455. For further details, see K G C Reid *The Abolition of Feudal Tenure in Scotland* (2003). Most of the rest of the Act – effecting actual abolition of the feudal system – comes into force on the 'appointed day', which has been confirmed as Martinmas (28 November) 2004. See the Abolition of Feudal Tenure etc (Scotland) Act 2000 (Commencement No 2) (Appointed Day) Order 2003, SSI 2003/456, and the Abolition of Feudal Tenure etc (Scotland) Act 2000 (Commencement No 3) Order 2003, SSI 2003/620.

Title Conditions (Scotland) Act 2003 (Consequential Provisions) Order 2003, SSI 2003/503

This amends a number of statutes, including both the Abolition of Feudal Tenure etc (Scotland) Act 2000 and the Title Conditions (Scotland) Act 2003. The changes are generally minor, although note should be taken of the amendments to s 20 of the 2000 Act to correct an error in earlier amendments made by the 2003 Act. See K G C Reid *The Abolition of Feudal Tenure in Scotland* (2003) para 3.33.

Listing of conservation bodies

An initial list of conservation bodies was made by the Title Conditions (Scotland) Act 2003 (Conservation Bodies) Order 2003, SSI 2003/453 (as amended, in respect of a mis-naming of the National Trust for Scotland, by the Title Conditions (Scotland) Act 2003 (Conservation Bodies) Amendment Order 2003, SSI 2003/621).

Superiors who are conservation bodies are able to preserve those feudal burdens which qualify as conservation burdens by registration of a notice under s 27 of the Abolition of Feudal Tenure etc (Scotland) Act 2000. Alternatively, it is possible, under s 27A, to preserve conservation burdens in favour of a third-party conservation body provided the body consents. Moreover, conservation burdens may be created of new in favour of conservation bodies by virtue of s 38 of the Title Conditions (Scotland) Act 2003.

The new statutory instruments list those bodies which qualify as conservation bodies. The complete list is:

- All local authorities
- Castles of Scotland Preservation Trust
- Edinburgh World Heritage Trust
- Glasgow Building Preservation Trust
- Highlands Buildings Preservation Trust
- Plantlife – The Wild-Plant Conservation Charity
- Scottish Natural Heritage
- Solway Heritage
- St Vincent Crescent Preservation Trust
- Strathclyde Building Preservation Trust
- The John Muir Trust
- The National Trust for Scotland for Places of Historic Interest or Natural Beauty
- The Royal Society for the Protection of Birds
- The Trustees of the Landmark Trust
- The Trustees of the New Lanark Conservation Trust
- The Woodland Trust.

The Scottish Ministers also are treated as a conservation body, by virtue of the primary legislation.

Lands Tribunal: rules and fees

New rules for the Lands Tribunal for Scotland, replacing many (but not all) of those currently contained in the Lands Tribunal for Scotland Rules 1971, SI 1971/218, are enacted by the Lands Tribunal for Scotland Rules 2003, SSI 2003/452. Among other matters, these provide rules, and forms, in relation to applications in respect of real burdens under the Abolition of Feudal Tenure etc (Scotland) Act 2000 and the Title Conditions (Scotland) Act 2003. Fees in respect of these applications, and certain other matters, are provided for by the Lands Tribunal for Scotland (Relevant Certificate) (Fees) Rules 2003, SSI 2003/451, and the Lands Tribunal for Scotland Amendment (Fees) Rules 2003, SSI 2003/521.

Compulsory purchase: new forms for CPOs and GVDs

The Compulsory Purchase of Land (Scotland) Regulations 2003, SSI 2003/446, prescribe the forms in which compulsory purchase orders and general vesting declarations are to be made, and also other incidental notices and advertisements. The new regulations replace the Compulsory Purchase of Land (Scotland) Regulations 1976, SI 1976/820, as from 1 November 2003. The replacement is primarily to take account of the treatment of real burdens and servitudes on compulsory purchase under ss 106 and 109 of the Title Conditions (Scotland) Act 2003. For further details, see the Scottish Executive's *Planning Circular 4 2003* (available on www.scotland.gov.uk/library5/planning/pc403-00.asp).

Housing (Scotland) Act 2001 (Transfer of Scottish Homes Property and Liabilities) Order 2003, SSI 2003/532

This statutory instrument transfers some (not all) properties and liabilities from Scottish Homes to the Scottish Ministers. The instrument is made under the Housing (Scotland) Act 2001 (asp 10).

Money laundering etc

During 2003 the Proceeds of Crime Act 2002 came into force. It repealed Part V of the Criminal Law (Consolidation) (Scotland) Act 1995, replacing it with new provisions. Also in 2003 the Money Laundering Regulations 2003, SI 2003/3075, came into force, replacing the Money Laundering Regulations 1993, SI 1993/1933 (as amended). The new regime is tougher than the old. The current Solicitors Accounts Rules (Solicitors (Scotland) Accounts, Accounts Certificate,

Professional Practice and Guarantee Fund Rules 2001) are tied to the old legislation and so will now need amendment. The Law Society of Scotland's website
(www.lawscot.org.uk) has a valuable text, *Simple Guide to Anti-Money Laundering
Regulations and Associated Legislation*. See also a note by Ken Swinton at (2003) 71
Scottish Law Gazette 45.

The case of *P v P* [2003] 3 WLR 1350 (English High Court), which turns on the
Proceeds of Crime Act 2002, has attracted considerable attention. See eg an article by Janice Jones in the *Journal of the Law Society for Scotland* for November 2003
(p 34). In a divorce case the wife's lawyers came to suspect that part of the husband's assets might have come from criminal activity. Section 328 of the 2002 Act
provides that:

(1) A person commits an offence if he enters into or becomes concerned in an arrangement which he knows or suspects facilitates (by whatever means) the acquisition,
retention, use or control of criminal property by or on behalf of another person.

(2) But a person does not commit such an offence if –

(a) he makes an authorised disclosure under section 338 and (if the disclosure is
made before he does the act mentioned in subsection (1)) he has the appropriate consent . . . .

The wife's lawyers made a report to the National Criminal Intelligence Service
(NCIS), reporting their suspicions and asking for guidance as to whether they
could inform either their own client, or the lawyers for the husband, of the problem. The reason for this latter concern is that the 2002 Act makes 'tipping off' an
offence (see ss 333 and 342). We quote from the judgment of Dame Elizabeth
Butler-Sloss (paras [4] and [5]):

The NCIS did not respond in writing to that letter. A number of telephone calls were
made by the wife's solicitors to the duty officer at NCIS, whose advice (which NCIS
now accepts was misleading) was that the decision to continue to act was purely a
'business decision' for the solicitors. The officer advised that a report was only required
if money were actually about to change hands. He also thought, however, that if the
money were not to pass through the solicitors' hands that a report might not be necessary at all. This advice was wrong. Crucially, the NCIS officer also advised that the
wife's solicitors were not permitted to tell either the other side, or their own client, that
the disclosure report had been made, as it would contravene the tipping off provisions
and/or the prohibition against prejudicing an investigation.

Having been instructed not to disclose the fact of their report to either the husband or
the wife, or to the husband's solicitors, the wife's solicitors felt that they were left in an
extremely difficult position. Further attempts to seek clarification from the NCIS
proved unsuccessful. Letters were sent on 25 June and 9 July, but by 15 July a response
had not been received.

Finding themselves in an impossible position, the wife's lawyers applied to the
court for guidance. At the hearing various parties were represented, including
the NCIS and the Law Society of England and Wales. Dame Butler-Sloss's judg-

ment has clarified a number of matters. It appears that the wife's solicitors were indeed bound to make the report to the NCIS. Agent-client confidentiality was irrelevant. However, ss 333 and 342 of the 2002 Act, which make tipping off an offence, have certain provisions in favour of solicitors acting as such.

This was a divorce case, but the issues are not confined to divorce, nor indeed to litigation of any sort. They apply equally in conveyancing, if any solicitor involved suspects that the buyer's funds may be tainted. Indeed, these issues also arise if either solicitor suspects that the property was itself acquired originally with tainted money.

Receivership, administration and irritancy

Section 248 of the Enterprise Act 2002 came into force on 15 September 2003. See the Enterprise Act 2002 (Commencement No 4 and Transitional Provisions and Savings) Order 2003, SI 2003/2093. The effect is that 'in Scotland, a landlord may not exercise a right of irritancy in relation to premises let to the company except– (a) with the administrator's consent, or (b) with the permission of the court'. See Schedule B1, para 43(5), of the Insolvency Act 1986 (as substituted by the 2002 Act).

For discussion see Alistair Duncan 'Irritancy and the Enterprise Act 2002' (2003) 66 *Greens Property Law Bulletin* 7.

Another effect of the 2002 Act is that any floating charge granted after 15 September 2003 cannot be enforced by receivership, unless it falls under one of the statutory exceptions. (See *Conveyancing 2002* pp 89–91.) However, Professor David Bennett has argued cogently that the Act's definitional structure is defective and that accordingly receivership may after all continue to be available for post-Act floating charges: see David A Bennett (2004) 67 *Greens Business Law Bulletin* 1.

Part III

Part III: Other material

Law of the tenement

In March 2003 the Scottish Executive published for consultation a draft Tenements (Scotland) Bill, substantially based on the Bill by the Scottish Law Commission included in its *Report on the Law of the Tenement* (Scot Law Com No 162, 1998). There was also published an empirical study of deeds of conditions: Ann Flint, James Barrowman and Derek O'Carroll *Modern Title and Condition Deeds in Scotland and their Effectiveness in Securing Common Repairs* (Scottish Executive Social Research, 2003). The Bill itself was introduced to the Scottish Parliament on 30 January 2004.

Foreshore and sea bed

In March 2003 the Scottish Law Commission published its final recommendations on reform of the law of the foreshore and sea bed: see *Report on Law of the Foreshore and Sea Bed* (Scot Law Com No 190, 2003; available on www.scotlawcom.gov.uk). Under the recommendations, existing public rights are to be rationalised and brought within the administrative framework established by the Land Reform (Scotland) Act 2003 in respect of access rights over land. Public rights, currently confined to the foreshore proper, are to be extended to the part of the beach lying landward of the foreshore.

Irritancy of leases

In June 2003 the Scottish Law Commission published its final recommendations on reform of the law of irritancy in leases: see *Report on Irritancy in Leases of Land* (Scot Law Com No 191, 2003; available on www.scotlandcom.gov.uk). While retaining much of the current framework of the law, the *Report* recommends better protection for tenants in the form of a more robust system of notices, and the extension of that protection to agricultural and residential leases. Under the recommendations it will cease to be possible to obtain immediate irritancy in the event of insolvency. Instead, and assuming the lease to be assignable, the landlord must allow the insolvency practitioner a period of at least six months in order to dispose of the lease. Only if no disposal takes place is irritancy permissible.

Housing Improvement Task Force

The Housing Improvement Task Force submitted its second report in 2003. See **Commentary** p 96.

Barony titles and armorial bearings

On 17 December 2002 the Lord Lyon King of Arms announced rules which he intended to operate in relation to feudal baronies following the abolition of the feudal system. In essence these provided that the Lord Lyon would no longer officially recognise a person as a feudal baron or make any grant of baronial additaments as part of armorial bearings. (The rules are reproduced on p 42 of *Conveyancing 2002*. See also K G C Reid *The Abolition of Feudal Tenure in Scotland* (2003) para 14.6.) It seems, however, that there has been a change of mind, for it has now been announced (see 2003 SLT (News) 244) that:

> As a result of representations which have been made the Lord Lyon has decided to give further consideration to the procedure to be applied in respect of feudal baronies after the appointed day. The rules announced on 17 December 2002 are, in the meantime, to be treated as suspended and subject to possible modification.

Despite the prospect of feudal abolition, the market for barony titles has remained robust, with sales almost doubling over the last two years. During 2003 alone Baronytitles.com sold 13 titles, mainly to Scottish expatriates and their descendants, at an average price of £55,000. See *The Scotsman* 30 December 2003.

Solicitors (Scotland) (Client Communication) (Residential Conveyancing) Practice Rules 2003

These rules came into force on 1 December 2003. They may be a response to the work of the Housing Improvement Action Task Force (discussed on p 86). The substance is to be found in rule 3:

> A solicitor shall at the earliest practical opportunity upon receiving instructions to undertake any residential conveyancing work on behalf of a private client, provide the following information to the client in writing:
>
> (a) details of such work to be carried out on behalf of the client;
>
> (b) either
>
> > (i) an estimate of the total fee to be charged for such work, including VAT and outlays which may be incurred in the course of such work; or
> >
> > (ii) the basis upon which a fee will be charged for such work, including VAT and outlays which may be incurred in the course of such work;
>
> (c) the identity of the person or persons who will principally carry out such work on behalf of the client; and
>
> (d) the identity of the person whom the client should contact if the client becomes concerned in any way with the manner in which such work is being carried out.

Failure to send such a letter at the outset is professional misconduct (rule 5). The Rules apply only to residential conveyancing for private clients. A 'private client' is 'an individual who instructs a solicitor otherwise than in the course of a business or profession' (rule 2(1)). The Rules speak of 'the client' in the singular. Where there are two or more clients (eg husband and wife) the prescribed information must be sent to them all. There is no requirement that the information be sent to each separately. So a single letter addressed to both (if living at the same address) would, it seems, suffice. If the client is a body of trustees there might be scope for debate as to whether the Rules would apply, since whilst the trustees themselves will be individuals (except for the case of a corporate trustee) they will not be acting as such. The safe course, however, is to send the standard letter to each trustee.

The Law Society of Scotland has issued a sample letter which can be used for the purpose of complying with the Rules: see *Journal of the Law Society* for November 2003 (p 47):

Dear [Name]

We refer to your recent meeting with [Name].

We are pleased to confirm that [the Firm] will be acting on your behalf in connection with [the work to be carried out].

The solicitor who will be dealing with your work on a day-to-day basis is [Name].

We will advise you at regular intervals regarding the progress of your work and keep you informed of all significant developments. If you are uncertain about what is happening at any time, please ask.

We enclose an Estimate of our Fees and Outlays for this transaction. If the work turns out to be more complex than normal, we may require to increase our estimate to take account of this. We will inform you as soon as possible about any such increase.

The Money Laundering Regulations require us to be satisfied as to the identity of our clients and as to the source of any funds passing through our hands. In order to comply with these Regulations, we may need to ask you for proof of identity and other information in relation to these matters. We reserve the right to withdraw from acting for you if you fail to provide us with the information requested of you and required in connection with our Money Laundering Procedures.

Finally, our aim is to provide a service which is satisfactory in every respect. However, if you have any concerns about the manner in which work is being carried out on your behalf, please contact our Client Relations Partner [Name] who will be happy to discuss your concerns.

Standard forms in commercial conveyancing

On the initiative of Dundas & Wilson, Maclay Murray & Spens, McGrigor Donald, and Shepherd + Wedderburn, a Property Standardisation Group has been established in order to produce agreed forms of documentation and of procedures. Thus far the Group has produced a due diligence questionnaire (for precontractual inquiries), a suite of letters of obligation (notably including lease transactions), and a completion checklist. All documentation, and further information, is available on www.psglegal.co.uk.

Coal mining reports

Coal mining reports from the Coal Authority are available online at www.coalminingreports.co.uk. They are now covered by insurance. The Authority's online directory provides immediate confirmation, by postcode, as to whether a search is recommended. A new service, for an additional fee, is an interpretative report, which includes a risk assessment as to whether the building in question is inside or outside the possible zone of ground movement from any reported mine entry. Further information, and a table of fees, are given in the *Journal of the Law Society of Scotland* for September 2003 (p 56).

Preservation of real burdens by superiors

Under Part 4 of the Abolition of Feudal Tenure etc (Scotland) Act 2000, which was brought into force on 1 November 2003, superiors are sometimes able to preserve the right to enforce real burdens. This requires the registration of an appropriate statutory notice before 28 November 2004. A comprehensive account will be found in K G C Reid *The Abolition of Feudal Tenure in Scotland* (2003). Guidance from the Keeper is given in the *Journal of the Law Society of Scotland* for November 2003 (p 58) and on www.ros.gov.uk. The most common notice – that under s 18 of the 2000 Act – requires to be registered against both the feu (the 'servient tenement') and also the property to which enforcement rights are to be reallotted (the 'dominant tenement'). Where one of these properties is in the Land Register and one in the Register of Sasines, the notice requires to be accompanied by application forms for both. Where both properties are on the Land Register, one Form 2 is sufficient, specifying both title numbers. Where both are in the Register of Sasines, one CPB2 is sufficient.

Registers of Scotland

All counties now operational areas

On 1 April 2003 the last remaining registration counties became operational for registration of title. See the Land Registration (Scotland) Act 1979 (Commencement No 16) Order 2002, SSI 2002/432. The counties in question were Banff, Caithness, Moray, Orkney and Zetland, Ross and Cromarty, and Sutherland. This means that all sales in Scotland now must be registered in the Land Register. Currently the Register comprises some 900,000 titles, which is a little under half of the potential final total. See *Journal of the Law Society of Scotland* for May 2003, p 68.

Reports by email

Reports (eg Form 10 reports) can be instructed, and transmitted, entirely by email via the eFORMS ONLINE service.

Foreshore in Orkney and Shetland

In the case of udal land, the owner's right in respect of the foreshore is taken to extend to the 'lowest ebb', which is likely to be a greater right than elsewhere in Scotland where the boundary is the low-water mark of ordinary spring tides. As the lowest ebb cannot be plotted precisely, title plans in Orkney and Shetland will show only the standard low-water mark, but the following note will be added:

> NOTE: The subjects in this title include foreshore. While the title plan shows the extent of the foreshore as being bounded by the mean low-water mark of ordinary spring tides, the subjects extend to the lowest ebb.

See *Journal of the Law Society of Scotland* for May 2003 p 69. As to whether ownership of the foreshore under udal law carries with it additional pertinents, such as bait within the ebb and hunting seal, see Scottish Law Commission *Report on Law of the Foreshore and Sea Bed* (Scot Law Com No 190, 2003; available on www.scotlawcom.gov.uk) paras 4.12 ff.

Exclusive garden ground in tenements

Helpful guidance is given for first registrations of a tenement flat where the applicant asserts exclusive ownership of a garden. See (2003) 71 *Scottish Law Gazette* 123-4. If the extent of the garden is given clearly in the Sasine title, a plan is not required. Instead the Sasine description will be reproduced on the title sheet. If the extent is unclear, there is a choice. A plan can be commissioned, and the Keeper will not exclude indemnity if this is accompanied either (1) by affidavits as to possession for the prescriptive period by the previous owner or owners of the flat; or (2) by letters of consent by the current owners of the other flats. If a plan is not used, the Keeper will use the Sasine description but under exclusion of indemnity in respect of location and extent.

Adults with Incapacity (Scotland) Act 2000

A note published at (2003) 71 *Scottish Law Gazette* 51 gives guidance in the light of experience in relation to various matters arising under the 2000 Act.

Conflicts of interest

Acting for both builders and purchasers

The following note appeared in the *Journal of the Law Society of Scotland* in March 2003 (p 9):

Rule 5(1) of the Solicitors (Scotland) Practice Rules 1986 (Conflict of Interest Rules) provides that where the seller of residential property is a builder or developer a solicitor will only be able to act for seller and purchaser where the purchaser is an associated company or where the parties are public authorities, public bodies, Government departments or agencies. From the time the rules came into force the Professional Practice Committee have been of the view that acting for the seller as estate agent only is acting at a stage for the seller even if all offers are to be submitted to a different firm of solicitors.

The Committee have recently reviewed this policy and have agreed that it can be relaxed where the solicitors are only providing an estate agency service to a builder or developer in respect of properties being sold at a fixed price with a standard missive which will be submitted to and negotiated with a different firm of solicitors. In these circumstances if an established client of the firm wishes to purchase one of the plots or houses the Committee will normally be willing to grant a waiver provided that the solicitors themselves are satisfied that there is no actual conflict of interest between the parties and that no advice on the value or price will be sought from the solicitor acting as estate agent.

Commercial security transactions

The Solicitors (Scotland) Practice Rules 1986 provide rules as to the avoidance of conflict of interest. The October issue (p 45) of the *Journal of the Law Society of Scotland* contains a statement by the Professional Practice Committee discussing the Rules in connection with clients borrowing for business purposes, and stressing that even in 'de minimis' cases separate representation may be advisable.

Debt arrangement schemes and standard securities

The Debt Arrangement and Attachment (Scotland) Act 2002 (asp 17) provides for the introduction of debt arrangement schemes ('DAS'). The Act gives only a basic framework, leaving the detail to a statutory instrument. Thus far the statutory instrument has not been passed, but it is expected that it will be passed soon. Once a DAS is in effect, the debts that it covers can no longer be enforced according to the original contractual terms but only in accordance with the terms of the DAS. It has been unclear whether debts secured by standard security could be brought into debt arrangement schemes. This now seems likely.

Mike Dailly criticises this approach in a valuable article: 'The Impact of the Debt Arrangement Scheme on Secured Debt' (2003) 53/54 *Greens Civil Practice Bulletin* 3. One of his arguments is that to include secured debts would be ineffective anyway, since the 2002 Act merely provides that debts covered by a DAS cannot be enforced by diligence, and, as he rightly observes, debts secured by standard security do not normally need to be enforced by diligence but can be enforced in other ways. We would tentatively incline to the opposite view. Section 4 of the 2002 Act says that 'where a debt payment programme has been approved ... the debts specified in the application for the approval ... shall be paid in accordance with the programme'. Arguably, therefore, if a secured debt is included, and if the debtor keeps up the payments that are specified in the DAS, there is no default. If so, the standard security cannot, for the time being, be enforced.

Longer-term fixed-rate mortgages

In April 2003 the Chancellor of the Exchequer commissioned Professor David Miles, of Imperial College London, to 'undertake analysis of supply and demand side factors limiting the development of the longer-term fixed-rate mortgage market in the UK to establish why the share of longer-term fixed-rate mortgages is so low compared to the United States and many other EU countries' and to 'examine whether there has been any market failure that has held back the market for longer-term fixed-rate mortgages'. He was asked to produce an interim report in 2003 and a final report in time for the 2004 budget. The interim report has duly appeared: see H M Treasury *The UK Mortgage Market: Taking a Longer-Term View (Interim Report)* (ISBN 0 947 81979 7; available at www.hm-treasury.gov.uk). Its approach is, of course, from the standpoint of economics, and as such of limited interest to the conveyancer, though it does contain statistics about the housing market. But while its details may be of limited interest, its very existence shows that the UK Government wishes to increase the use of longer-term fixed-rate mortgages. For this purpose 'longer term' means ten years or more. Significant changes in mortgage packages may be on the way.

Mortgage arrears and repossessions

The Scottish Executive Development Department has published a report by Emma McCallum and Ewen McCaig on *Mortgage Arrears and Repossession* (ISBN 0 755 93500 4).

Books

George Bett *The Scottish Building Regulations Explained and Illustrated* (2003) (Blackwell Science; ISBN 0 632 04945 6)

Vincent Brown *Environmental Pollution Law and Commercial Transactions* (2003) (LexisNexis; ISBN 0 406 92758 8)

Malcolm Fleming, Julie McKinley and Alan McMillan *Dilapidations in Scotland* (2nd edn, 2003) (W Green; ISBN 0 414 01513 4)

T G Guthrie *Scottish Property Law* (2nd edn, 2003) (LexisNexis; ISBN 0 406 96358 4)

T Mullen *Homelessness and the Law* (2003) (Legal Services Agency, Glasgow)

William Neilson *Residential Care Fees – Defend the Assets* (3rd edn, 2003) (Spinning Acorn Ltd; ISBN 0 954 00420 5)

Kenneth Reid *The Abolition of Feudal Tenure in Scotland* (2003) (LexisNexis; ISBN 0 406 96968 X)

Kenneth Reid and George Gretton *Conveyancing 2002* (2003) (LexisNexis; ISBN 0 406 96664 8)

Robert Rennie *Land Tenure Reform* (2003) (W Green; ISBN 0 414 01549 5)

Jeremy Rowan-Robinson *Compulsory Purchase and Compensation* (2nd edn, 2003) (W Green; ISBN 0 414 01468 5)

Articles

A D Anderson 'The "Right to Roam" on Golf Courses' (2003) 71 *Scottish Law Gazette* 12

Nick Atkins 'Contaminated Land – Update' (2003) 64 *Greens Property Law Bulletin* 3

Alan Barr 'Bridging the Care Gap: *Robertson v Fife Council* and Paying for Residential Care' (2003) 7 *Edinburgh Law Review* 118

Alan Barr 'All Change for Stamp Duty' (2003) 48 *Journal of the Law Society of Scotland* Sept/28

David A Bennett 'Can Administrative Receivers Live On in Scotland?' (2004) 67 *Greens Business Law Bulletin* 1

Stewart Brymer 'Purchaser's Information Packs' (2003) 63 *Greens Property Law Bulletin* 4

Stewart Brymer 'Low Upset Prices' (2003) 64 *Greens Property Law Bulletin* 6 and 65 *Greens Property Law Bulletin* 7

David Cabrelli 'The Introduction of Stamp Duty Land Tax in Scotland' (2003) 66 *Greens Property Law Bulletin* 3

David Cabrelli 'Who Said Tax Doesn't Need to be Taxing? A Scottish Perspective on the Introduction of the Stamp Duty Land Tax and its Interaction with the Enterprise Act 2002' 2003 *Juridical Review* 277

James Connolly 'The Title Conditions (Scotland) Act 2003 and Servitudes' (2003) 8 *Scottish Law and Practice Quarterly* 217.

Conveyancing Committee of the Law Society of Scotland 'Clarifying the Classic Letter of Obligation' (2003) 48 *Journal of the Law Society of Scotland* April/26

Mike Dailly 'MRA: The Debtor's Perspective' (2003) 52 *Greens Civil Practice Bulletin* 3

Mike Dailly 'The Impact of the Debt Arrangement Scheme on Secured Debt' (2003) 53/54 *Greens Civil Practice Bulletin* 3 (reprinted at 2004 *SCOLAG* 6)

Ian A Davis 'Automated Registration of Title' (2003) 65 *Greens Property Law Bulletin* 5

Alistair Duncan 'Irritancy and the Enterprise Act' (2003) 66 *Greens Property Law Bulletin* 7

Sandra Eden 'Cautionary Tales – the Continued Development of *Smith v Bank of Scotland*' (2003) 7 *Edinburgh Law Review* 107

Alasdair Fox 'How the Leopard Changed its Spots' (2003) 48 *Journal of the Law Society of Scotland* May/58 (discussing the Agricultural Holdings (Scotland) Act 2003)

Alasdair Fox 'New Rights for Farm Tenants' (2003) 48 *Journal of the Law Society of Scotland* Dec/55

Caroline James 'Conveyancing Aspects of Cross-Border Transactions' (2003) 48 *Journal of the Law Society of Scotland* March/20

Patricia McKellar and Moira MacMillan with Catherine Cumming 'The E-Conveyancing Matrix' (2003) 8 *Scottish Law and Practice Quarterly* 95.

Keng Meng Khoo 'The Statutory Basis and Distribution of Ownership in Strata Titles and Tenement Schemes: A Singapore-Malaysia-Scotland Comparative Study' (2003) 8 *Scottish Law and Practice Quarterly* 9.

Linsey J Lewin 'The Art of Communication' (2003) 62 *Greens Property Law Bulletin* 3

Linsey J Lewin 'Commonsense Approach to Contaminated Land' (2003) 48 *Journal of the Law Society of Scotland* April/30

Linsey J Lewin 'Housing Improvement Task Force' (2003) 48 *Journal of the Law Society of Scotland* Nov/60 and Dec/62

Ian McFarlane 'Some Tax Essentials for Property Lawyers' (2003) 62 *Greens Property Law Bulletin* 5

Elaine Morris 'A Lender's View of E-Conveyancing' (2003) 65 *Greens Property Law Bulletin* 4

Elspeth Reid 'Personal Bar: Case-Law in Search of Principle' (2003) 7 *Edinburgh Law Review* 340

Robert Rennie 'A Matter of Opinion' (2003) 48 *Journal of the Law Society of Scotland* May/32

Robert Rennie 'The End of Conveyancing As We Know It' (2003) 48 *Journal of the Law Society of Scotland* Nov/15

Kenneth Ross 'Contaminated Land – Advice for Conveyancers' (2003) 71 *Scottish Law Gazette* 141

Kenneth Ross 'Issue of Contaminated Land must be Discussed with Clients' (2003) 48 *Journal of the Law Society of Scotland* May/65

Jonathan Seddon 'A Brief Look at Collateral Warranty Agreements' (2003) 63 *Greens Property Law Bulletin* 1

Jonathan Seddon 'Construction Procurement – An Introduction for Property Lawyers' (2003) 64 *Greens Property Law Bulletin* 1

Jonathan Seddon 'The use of "Standard Forms" in Construction Law – Some Pitfalls' (2003) 65 *Greens Property Law Bulletin* 1

Jonathan Seddon 'The Role of Professional Indemnity Insurers in Construction Contracts' (2003) 66 *Greens Property Law Bulletin* 1

Andrew Steven 'Implied Enforcement Rights in relation to Real Burdens in terms of the Title Conditions (Scotland) Act 2003' (2003) 71 *Scottish Law Gazette* 146

Andrew Steven and Alan Barr 'The Land Reform (Scotland) Act 2003 (Part 1)' (2003) 66 *Greens Property Law Bulletin* 5

John Stirling 'A Changing Duty to Wives' (2003) 53/54 *Greens Civil Practice Bulletin* 7

Ken Swinton 'Stamp Duty Land Tax: Are you Ready for the Changes?' (2003) 71 *Scottish Law Gazette* 165

Ken Swinton 'Single Survey Pilots' (2003) 71 *Scottish Law Gazette* 177

Ken Swinton 'Real Burdens After Feudal Abolition' (2003) 71 *Scottish Law Gazette* 188

Joe Thomson 'Limiting *Smith*' (2003) 71 *Scottish Law Gazette* 158 (on *Smith v Bank of Scotland* 1997 SC (HL) 111 and *Royal Bank of Scotland v Wilson* 2003 SC 544)

Andrew Wade 'Cracking the Code' (2003) 62 *Greens Property Law Bulletin* 6 and 63 *Greens Property Law Bulletin* 3

Scott Wortley 'Preserving Feudal Burdens as Praedial Real Burdens: Reallotment under the Abolition of Feudal Tenure etc (Scotland) Act 2000' (2003) 71 *Scottish Law Gazette* 73

Part IV

Part IV: Commentary

Missives of sale

Suspensive conditions: protecting the buyer

Suspensive conditions are good for buyers but bad for sellers. For buyers they offer opportunity without commitment. For sellers they amount to commitment without certainty. Suspensive conditions often function virtually as purchase options. But whereas no one would grant an overt option without payment, owners are oddly prepared to enter into suspended missives without payment. Whether the sale goes ahead depends on the vigour with which the buyer pursues an application for planning permission, or a liquor licence, or other matter in respect of which the condition is made; and in the meantime the seller is committed to a sale which may never take place.[1] Wise sellers protect their position by insisting on a timetable in the missives for purification of the condition. But, as three new cases show, the drafting of a suitable clause is not free from difficulty.

In *Miller Group Ltd v Park's of Hamilton (Holdings) Ltd*[2] a site was acquired for housing, and the bargain turned on whether planning permission could be obtained on satisfactory terms. In terms of missives the planning application was to be made within 12 weeks. Thereafter it was to be pursued 'with all due diligence'. In the event of an actual or deemed refusal there was to be an appeal within four weeks provided that there were realistic prospects of success. But what if the purchaser slipped up in this timetable? Was the bargain then at an end, or was the seller bound to allow further time? It was this issue that was the subject of litigation.

There was a deemed refusal of planning permission, followed by a failure to appeal during the stipulated four weeks. The seller purported to rescind the contract. Its right to do so was challenged. The seller relied on the following provision of missives:

> Should the Purchaser decide that there is no realistic prospect of success of such appeal and therefore decide within said four-week period not to lodge an appeal as aforesaid then the Seller shall be entitled to rescind the missives without penalty.

But this provision did not cover all the possibilities. In particular it did not cover the possibility that had actually arisen, namely that, without regard to prospects

---

1 G L Gretton and K G C Reid *Conveyancing* (2nd edn, 1999) paras 3.19 and 3.21.
2 *Miller Group Ltd v Park's of Hamilton (Holdings) Ltd* 2003 GWD 8-225.

of success, the purchaser had simply *delayed* in appealing. In the absence of express provision, the court held, matters were governed by the general law. Indeed the very fact that provision had been made for one situation showed that in other situations the parties had left matters to that law.[1] Under the general law, time was not of the essence. It was true, of course, that there had been a breach of contract (ie a failure to appeal timeously). But, on normal principles, the seller must give the purchaser a reasonable time in which to perform. Only then could it rescind.[2] But by then it would be too late, for the immediate response of the purchaser to the purported rescission had been to exercise its contractual right to waive the suspensive condition. Subject to the results of an eventual proof, the seller was therefore locked into the bargain.

An instructive contrast is provided by *Campbell v Ferguson, MacSween & Stewart*.[3] Here too there were suspensive conditions, one about planning permission, but in other respects the missives were more even-handed as between the parties. In particular, the time for purification of the conditions had a limit:

> With regard to Conditions 5 and 14 of your client's offer of 31 October 1994 in the event that these conditions are not both purified or waived by the purchaser with a period of six months from the date of conclusion of missives then our clients shall be free to resile from these missives and that without any penalty due to or by either party.

Under this clause the balance of rights was delicate. The purchasers could insist on the bargain if either they obtained planning permission etc or alternatively waived the conditions. Otherwise, once the six-month period had passed, the sellers could withdraw. It would be important to keep an eye on the clock, for if purification was not in immediate prospect the purchasers would have to waive the conditions in order to make sure of the acquisition. In the event, the sellers purported to resile from the contract before the conditions had either been purified or waived.

The dispute, curiously, was about the meaning of 'date of conclusion of missives', which was the starting point for the six-month period. This was a transaction in which missives were repeatedly concluded and then reopened again by further missive letters. The question for decision was whether the relevant date was (1) the date when the bargain was concluded for the last time, or (2) the date when the bargain was concluded with the clause in question. If the answer was (2), the six-month period had expired and the sellers could resile. If it was (1), the six-month period had not expired and the purchasers could thwart the sellers by waiving the conditions. The action was in fact fought, not between the purchasers and sellers, but between the purchasers and their allegedly negligent solicitors. It was held that the proper interpretation was (1), and that accordingly the purported withdrawal from the contract was ineffective.

---

1 2003 GWD 8-225 at para [15] per Lord Mackay of Drumadoon.
2 G L Gretton and K G C Reid *Conveyancing* (2nd edn, 1999) para 5.04.
3 *Campbell v Ferguson, MacSween & Stewart* 2003 GWD 14-463.

A third case about suspensive conditions is *Bluestone Estates Ltd v Fitness First Clubs Ltd*.[1] As in the case just discussed, the missives contained an escape clause: if planning permission was not obtained by 31 December 2001 either party could resile without penalty. But unlike the previous two cases, it was the purchasers and not the sellers who were interested in withdrawing. Planning permission was delayed and was not obtained until 20 March 2002. A month later the purchasers purported to resile. Their real motive, it appears, was not to back out but to negotiate a lower price. The sellers resisted the rescission on the basis of personal bar. By delaying by four months, they argued, the purchasers had impliedly waived any right to rescind. Unsurprisingly, the argument did not succeed. A mere delay in insisting on a right does not, of itself, constitute personal bar. There must also be 'indicators of unfairness', for example prejudice to the other party due to the delay.[2] In *Bluestone Estates* the prejudice was slight and the delay itself relatively short. Accordingly, the purchasers were free to resile and seek a lower price.

In *Bluestone Estates* the purchasers were entitled to rescind even though the condition had been satisfied, out of time. Here there may be a difference between suspensive conditions and ordinary conditions. With the former, satisfaction of the condition does not prevent rescission in a case where time was of the essence. With ordinary conditions, however, rescission may be barred, although authority is divided.[3] In one case, for example, a seller was unable to rescind for non-payment once payment had been tendered, notwithstanding that it was tendered late and that, in terms of the missives, punctual payment was of the essence of the contract.[4] The difference, if there is one, is between rescission for breach and rescission for non-purification. A suspensive condition does not, of itself, impose obligations on the parties. It merely nominates an event, largely outside the control of either party, which must occur in order for the contract to take effect. But in an ordinary condition, the right to rescind arises directly from a breach (such as non-payment of the price), and may disappear, following performance, with the breach itself.

Defective central heating

In *Williams v Mutter*[5] the pursuer bought a house from the defenders. When, after entry, he tried out the central heating system, he found that the radiators did not become properly hot. The matter was covered in the missives, clause 13 of the offer providing that:

---

1 *Bluestone Estates Ltd v Fitness First Clubs Ltd* 2003 GWD 27-768.
2 Elspeth Reid 'Personal Bar: Case Law in Search of Principle' (2003) 7 *Edinburgh Law Review* 340, 348 ff.
3 See G L Gretton and K G C Reid *Conveyancing* (2nd edn, 1999) para 3.26.
4 *Cumming v Brown* 1994 SLT (Sh Ct) 11. But compare *Ford Sellar Morris Properties plc v E W Hutchison Ltd* 1990 SC 34.
5 *Williams v Mutter* 2002 SCLR 1127.

> The central heating system and all associated equipment ... [is] in full and efficient working order ... and any fault intimated to the seller within seven days of entry will be corrected at the expense of the seller.

Following his discovery the pursuer immediately arranged for his solicitor to write to the defenders' agents in the following terms:

> Our clients have advised that the central heating system within the property is defective. There is no heat being generated and the boiler is losing pressure. Further, it appears that the thermostat in the lounge is not connected. Our clients have asked Scottish Gas to carry out an inspection and provide a report and we will let you have a copy as soon as available. In the meantime, please treat this letter as intimation of the defect in terms of the missives and let us have your clients' comments.

The defects proved worse than was first feared, and in the end it was necessary to replace the pipework and the radiators at considerable expense. The defenders disputed liability. Properly read, they argued, clause 13 covered only such *specific defects* as were intimated within seven days. But the defects so intimated did not include the radiators and pipework. Hence they did not fall within clause 13.

Like most provisions in missives, clause 13 looks less impressive with hindsight. No doubt there *was* something in the defenders' argument, and matters would have been clearer had the clause required only intimation in general terms. Was the letter sufficient? The sheriff principal[1] held that it was. In his opinion, the warranty itself was in general terms, so that any intimation needed only to be in general terms as well. It was wrong to read into clause 13 a requirement to specify the precise defects, and a limitation that only defects so specified could be repaired.

Following this decision it may be worth reviewing the wording of this standard clause. The interests of buyers and sellers are not identical. Buyers will want to be able to intimate simply that the heating does not work properly. Sellers will be wary of a clause which allows a merely general assertion, for fear that such assertions come to be made routinely as a means of avoiding the substance of the seven-day rule.

Leases

Keep-open clauses

Back in the 1990s one of the major issues in the law of commercial leases was the efficacy of keep-open clauses, ie clauses which not only require the tenant to occupy, but also to keep trading. Could such clauses be specifically enforced? In England it was decided that specific performance was not normally available:

---

1   R A Dunlop QC.

Co-operative Insurance v Argyll Stores Ltd.[1] In Scotland things went the other way and specific implement is normally available: *Highland and Universal Properties Ltd v Safeway Properties Ltd.*[2] Since the law was clarified by those decisions, litigation has become much rarer. *Oak Mall Greenock Ltd v McDonald's Restaurants Ltd*[3] is thus a rarity. It concerned a unit in the Oak Mall Shopping Centre in Greenock. The lease was for 25 years, from 1997 to 2022. The lease provided that the unit was to be used

> only as a quick service restaurant for consumption of food and non-alcoholic drink both on and off the Leased Premises and for the sale of any related items with ancillary storage, staff and office accommodation or for such purpose within Class 1 of the Schedule to the Town and Country Planning (Use Classes) (Scotland) Order 1989.

The tenant was bound

> to carry on such business as is permitted by Clause 4.12.1 or procure the same to be carried on in a proper and normal manner and to keep the Leased Premises open for trade for not less than the normal shopping hours of the Centre.

But it was provided that the clause just quoted

> shall not require the Tenant to occupy or trade from the Leased Premises if ... the Tenant is ... effecting a disposal by the Tenant of its interest ... whether by way of assignation or sub-letting (provided that the party in whom the Tenant's interest is vested from time to time shall not be entitled to vacate the Leased Premises while effecting a disposal as aforesaid for longer than three months during the period when the Tenant's interest is vested in such party).

What happened cannot be told better than in the words of the Lord Ordinary (Drummond Young):[4]

> On or about 9 September 2001 the defenders ceased carrying on their business from the units that form the subjects of let. No prior warning was given to the pursuers of their intention to cease trading. Property agents acting for the pursuers wrote to the defenders on 12 September 2001 demanding to know why the defenders were refusing to comply with their obligations ... The defenders intimated that they were exercising their option in terms of clause 4.12.2 ... not to open for business while effecting a disposal of their interest in the units. By letter dated 3 December 2001, property agents for the pursuers notified the defenders that in terms of the Lease they were bound to re-open by 9 December 2001. The pursuers' solicitors wrote to the defenders on 7 December 2001 seeking confirmation that they would resume occupation ... By letter dated 12 December 2001, solicitors for the defenders intimated that it was not the

1 *Co-operative Insurance v Argyll Stores Ltd* [1998] AC 1.
2 *Highland and Universal Properties Ltd v Safeway Properties Ltd* 2000 SC 297, 2000 SLT 414.
3 *Oak Mall Greenock Ltd v McDonald's Restaurants Ltd* 2003 GWD 17-540.
4 2003 GWD 17-540 at para [2].

defenders' intention to re-occupy the premises. The defenders have not conducted business from the units and have not opened them for business since that date.

The landlord sought to enforce the keep-open clause by specific implement. In view of *Highland and Universal Properties Ltd v Safeway Properties Ltd* the landlord evidently had a strong prima facie case. The defender advanced four arguments against specific implement. Again in the words of the Lord Ordinary:[1]

> *First*, they argued that the provisions of clause 4.12.1 and .2 were not such as to be appropriate for specific implement. *Secondly*, they argued that the court should refuse to grant specific implement in the terms sought, because that would involve innovating upon the parties' contract. *Thirdly*, they argued that the court has an underlying discretion to refuse specific implement in the particular circumstances of the case, and that that discretion should be exercised in the defenders' favour in the present case. *Fourthly*, they argued that the pursuers, through their actings, had waived their right to insist on the three months' time limit that applied to the provisions in clause 4.12.2 authorising the disposal of the tenant's interest in the lease; consequently the defenders were still entitled to seek to dispose of their interest, and were entitled not to occupy while they were doing so.

All four arguments were rejected and we will comment only on the first, which was really a re-run of the argument advanced in earlier cases, namely that a decree of specific implement has to be clear as to what the defender is required to do, but the terms of the lease were too vague. There is a certain irony in McDonald's, the defender, asserting that it did not know what a 'quick service restaurant' is. More generally, we would suggest that if a contractual provision is sufficiently clear that breach will give rise to damages – and that standard of clarity is generally met – then it is sufficiently clear for specific implement. The reason is simple. In either case the question is the same: has the obligation been complied with or not? If breach can be established in the one case it can be established in the other.

An earthquake that did not happen

Allied Dunbar Assurance plc v Superglass Sections Ltd[2] was an earthquake that did not happen: that is to say, the pursuer adduced an argument which had a certain degree of theoretical cogency and which, had it succeeded, would have turned a good deal of the law of leases upside down.

The pursuer was the head landlord of commercial property at Clydebank Business Park, Clydebank. The defender held under a 20-year sub-lease granted in 1991. The lease contained certain break options. In February 2001 the tenant duly exercised one of the break options so as to bring the lease to an end at

---

1 2003 GWD 17-540 at para [4].
2 *Allied Dunbar Assurance plc v Superglass Sections Ltd* 2003 GWD 36-1013.

11 November 2001. There then ensued a dispute about whether the property was in the state of repair required by the lease – a subject always known by the curious name of 'dilapidations'. Needless to say, the landlord said that the property was in disrepair while the tenant took the opposite position. The landlord sued. Thus far, the case was purely factual. But the landlord also sought declarator that since the tenant was (allegedly) in breach of its repairing obligations, it could not found on its exercise of the break option. This idea seems odd at first sight, but is not without a certain logic. A contracting party who is in breach cannot normally insist that the counterparty perform. As counsel for the pursuer argued, all this followed from the mutuality principle in the law of contract.

The Lord Ordinary (Lord Eassie) rejected this argument, surely rightly. As he observed:[1]

> If valid, the pursuers' proposition that the existence of a material breach of contract on the part of the tenant at the ish results in the continuing of the tenancy must have wider, general application. The converse must also logically apply, namely that a breach by a landlord of his obligations – eg a failure to repair or maintain the common parts of a shopping centre – would entitle the tenant to remain in occupation, notwithstanding the expiry of the term of the lease. As counsel for the defenders pointed out, there is no trace of any such doctrine in the law of landlord and tenant. And understandably so. For there is then no clarity or certainty as to the duration of the rights of occupancy.

And he continued:[2]

> Where a lease has come to an end at its expiry date, there can be no mutuality respecting some future continuation of the right or obligation of occupation. The right or obligation of occupancy has simply terminated. Viewed from another perspective, the present defenders do not seek to assert any right of possession or continuing occupation. They have yielded possession in terms of the provisions of the contract relating to duration of occupation and possession. They do not seek implement of any term of the contract involving any performance by the pursuers. Accordingly, even if the mutuality principle may be given the wider extent suggested by counsel for the pursuers of debarring a party in breach of one term of the contact from suing for implement of the right given to him by another term of the contract, unrelated to the obligation breached (which would not readily accord with the modern authorities), that argument fails for the simple reason that the defenders are, indeed, defenders advancing no claim. The principle of mutuality of contractual obligation is essentially a defence. It involves a riposte. In my opinion it cannot be subverted into the imposition of an additional contractual obligation to continue possession of the property, after the expiration of the lease, and to pay rent for that indefinite continuation.

---

1 2003 GWD 36-1013 at para [13].
2 2003 GWD 36-1013 at para [14].

Rent review clauses

Rent review clauses are hard to draft. Mistakes are easy and can be expensive. Two recent cases involved clauses with a literal reading that was absurd, and disastrous for one party. In one, the court felt able to disregard the literal meaning. In the other the opposite happened. The cases are classic 'interpretation of contract' cases, and their different results perhaps show that the interpretation of contracts is an unpredictable business.

The first case was *Howgate Shopping Centre Ltd v Catercraft Services Ltd*.[1] R Mathieson & Sons Ltd ('Mathieson') had a 99-year lease of a unit in Falkirk's Howgate shopping centre. The initial rent was low, and the rent review clause provided that every five years the market rental would be determined, and then the lessee would have to pay only 23% of that rental. So throughout the lease there would be rent reviews but the tenant would pay only 23% of market rate. The reason for this unusual provision was that Mathieson had owned some of the land on which the whole development took place, and part of the price for conveying it to the developer was that the company would receive a lease at below-market rates. After some time the company decided to sub-let. It granted a 25-year sub-lease to the defender. This sub-lease was at a full commercial rent, but it contained the following provision:

> the rent payable in terms of this Sub-Lease shall be subject to review on the 13th April 1995 and at Five yearly intervals thereafter and that in every case in accordance with the whole conditions, provisions and stipulations imposed upon and undertaken by the Tenant[2] in favour of the Landlord[3] and contained in Schedule Part IV of the Lease.[4]

In other words, the sub-lease imported the rent review provisions of the head lease. But the latter provided that the rent payable was 23% of the market rent. A literal reading of the sub-lease would mean that the sub-rent also would be 23% of the market sub-rent. The issue did not arise immediately, for the opening rent under the sub-lease was agreed at £55,000, but the problem came into focus on the first rent review for the sub-lease. The pursuer (Mathieson's successor in the mid-lease) sought declarator that the rent under the sub-lease fell to be ascertained by market rates, without being discounted down to 23%. In the event of being unsuccessful it also sought judicial rectification of the sub-lease.[5] It was, however, successful in the declarator.

The Lord Ordinary (Macfadyen) gave a long and careful opinion. One suspects that on the one hand he felt that the defender's position was cogent, while on the other hand his sense of justice rebelled against the result that a literal approach would produce.

---

1 *Howgate Shopping Centre Ltd v Catercraft Services Ltd* 2004 SLT 231.
2 That is, Mathieson.
3 That is, Mathieson's landlord.
4 That is, the lease in favour of Mathieson.
5 An increasingly common alternative.

The other case was *City Wall Properties (Scotland) Ltd v Pearl Assurance plc.*[1] The lease was of property at East Green Vaults under Aberdeen's Market Street. The property was a car park. The rent review clause provided:

> The rent so payable shall be subject to review at the instance of the Landlords at the relevant review date by addition per space of the product of 96 multiplied by 'the car park factor' (as hereinafter defined) applying at the relevant review date. For the purposes of the Lease 'the car park factor' shall mean the average of increased daily rates (ie the 9 hour rate from 0830 to 1730 hours charged to the public) at the Trinity Centre, Bon Accord Centre and the multi-storey College Street public car parks in Aberdeen . . . .

It is clear what the intention must have been. The rent would be increased so as to track increases at the comparator car parks. But is this what the clause actually says? Does 'the car park factor' mean (1) the average increase at the comparator car parks, or (2) the total new average rent at the comparator car parks? Thus suppose that the average comparator rate increased over the review period from £10 to £11. Would the 'car park factor' then be (1) £1 or (2) £11? On the actual figures in the case, the first interpretation would have produced a new rental of £37,774, whereas the second would have produced a new rental of £64,083 – about 70% higher. The second interpretation seems absurd, but it also is the literal meaning of the clause, and the Lord Ordinary (Clarke) felt unable to depart from that meaning.

Assignation and confusion

The *Howgate* case[2] raised another issue in the law of leases. The shopping centre was subject to three levels of lease, namely a head-lease, a mid-lease and a sub-lease. That involved four parties, and four real rights: the owner, the head-lessee, the mid-lessee and the sub-lessee. The head-lease was originally held by Meritclass Investments Ltd. The mid-lease was originally held by Mathieson. Meritclass assigned the head-lease to Xebec Investments Ltd. Xebec later assigned the head-lease to Howgate Shopping Centre Ltd ('Howgate'). Howgate later assigned the head-lease to Howgate Three Limited and Howgate Four Limited, who were second and third pursuers.[3] In addition, Mathieson assigned the mid-lease to Howgate. The result was that Howgate held, at least at one stage, both the head-lease and the mid-lease. Did this mean that the mid-lease disappeared by operation of *confusio*, ie automatic consolidation? And if so what effect did that have on the sub-lease?

The Lord Ordinary held that 'the same person cannot be both the landlord and the tenant of particular heritable subjects . . . Thus, when the landlord's and the

1 *City Wall Properties (Scotland) Ltd v Pearl Assurance plc* 2003 GWD 27-769.
2 *Howgate Shopping Centre Ltd v Catercraft Services Ltd* 2004 SLT 231.
3 The case proceeded on the basis that these various assignations were legally effective. But it seems that the head-lease was recorded in the Register of Sasines but none of the assignations, making it difficult to see how Meritclass Investments Ltd was ever divested of the head-lease.

tenant's interests come to be held by the same person, "the lesser right is absorbed into the greater right and is extinguished"'.[1] He also held that this fact could not affect the sub-lease. 'The sub-tenants remained in a contractual relationship with the party who had succeeded to the tenant's interest in the [mid-]lease'.[2] Despite his approval of the word 'extinguished' the Lord Ordinary reserved his opinion as to whether the lesser right is extinguished or merely suspended. The idea of suspension is problematic. Does it mean that the lease survives but that the obligations under it are unenforceable for the time being? However, the second point – that sub-leases are unaffected even by complete consolidation – seems sound and clear.

These issues are discussed in a valuable opinion of Professor Halliday's.[3] His view was that there is no automatic consolidation for registered leases. This opinion was cited to the court, but without success. However, the Lord Ordinary quoted with approval Halliday's remark that 'it makes no sense that valid sub-leases or heritable securities created over registered leases can be extinguished by the lessee acquiring the property, a transaction to which neither the sub-tenants nor the heritable creditors are parties'.[4] This consideration, it may be observed, is applicable whenever there is a consolidation, regardless of whether the possibility of automatic consolidation is accepted or not. We would observe, however, that if there is consolidation, the protection of sub-leases and of securities over the main lease must work in different ways. There is no insuperable difficulty in saying that the sub-lessees become direct lessees of the owner. But it makes no sense to say that what were securities over the lease become securities over the property itself. How this problem is to be solved is unclear. With considerable hesitation we would suggest that consolidation cannot take place without the consent of the holder of such a security. Valuable though the present case is, we venture to say that the whole subject remains subject to considerable difficulties.

Leases, servitudes and real burdens

Ultra-long leases (eg for 999 years[5]) are unusual but far from unknown.[6] They are, as it were, quasi-feus.[7] They fit awkwardly into the general law, which has not adapted to accommodate them. One illustration of this appears when a long leaseholder wishes to grant a servitude or real burden.

---

1 *Howgate Shopping Centre Ltd v Catercraft Services Ltd* 2004 SLT 231 at para [59]. The words quoted by the Lord Ordinary are those of Lord Hope in *Clydesdale Bank v Davidson* 1998 SC (HL) 51.

2 2004 SLT 231 at para [60].

3 Douglas J Cusine (ed) *The Conveyancing Opinions of Professor J M Halliday* (1992) p 377.

4 *The Conveyancing Opinions of Professor J M Halliday* p 380.

5 Why leases should be 99 or 999 years rather than 100 or 1,000 is a mystery to the authors.

6 Leases of residential property for more than 20 years are banned by the Land Tenure Reform (Scotland) Act 1974, s 8, and leases of any sort for more than 175 years by the Abolition of Feudal Tenure etc (Scotland) Act 2000, s 67. But these provisions do not affect leases created before the legislation came into force.

7 As such there are plans to convert them into simple ownership, as with feus: see Scottish Law Commission *Discussion Paper on Conversion of Long Leases* (Scot Law Com DP No 112, 2001; available on www.scotlawcom.gov.uk).

Suppose that there is a plot of land held on a 999-year lease created in, say, 1787. The title entered the Register of Sasines in the late nineteenth century and has perhaps now recently entered the Land Register. The leaseholder (Margaret) sells part of the ground (to Rory), and wishes to impose the usual sorts of burdens and servitudes that are found in split-off deeds. Can this be done? In fact it is impossible to create burdens or servitudes between the two plots, for two reasons. One is that both are owned by the same person – the landlord. Servitudes and real burdens can exist only between properties that are in separate hands. That problem is fatal. But equally fatal is the fact that rights in land can, in general, only be granted by the owner.[1] So no real burdens can be imposed on Rory's plot in favour of Margaret's plot. Might they be imposed, not on Rory's plot itself, but on his part of the leasehold, so that the burdens and servitudes would bind, not indeed the owner, but Rory's successors in title, for the duration of the lease? These would be, so to speak, quasi-burdens and quasi-servitudes. That too appears to be impossible, at least at common law.[2]

Traditionally the difficulty was usually ignored. Margaret would grant a break-off assignation, and this would contain the various servitudes and real burdens. Rory would record his deed in the Register of Sasines. Everyone would assume that the provisions were valid. But they were not.

The problem was addressed in 1985 by s 3 of the Law Reform (Miscellaneous Provisions) (Scotland) Act 1985. This inserted into the Registration of Leases (Scotland) Act 1857 the following new provision, s 3(2):

> It shall be, and shall be deemed always to have been, competent in an assignation under this section to impose conditions and make stipulations which, upon the recording of such assignation or the registration under the Land Registration (Scotland) Act 1979 of the assignee's interest, shall be as effectual against any singular successor of the assignee in the subjects assigned as if such assignee had been a grantee of the lease.

There can be no doubt as to the general idea. It was to address the difficulty identified above. And the provision perhaps looks fairly reasonable until one gets to the last phrase: 'as if such assignee had been a grantee of the lease'. But at this point the problems begin.[3]

First, the provision deems Rory to have been a grantee of the lease back in 1787. But even if Rory is deemed to have been alive in 1787 does that mean that the 1787 lease is deemed to have been granted, not to the actual grantee, but to Rory? If so, what are the consequences? This problem becomes the sharper the more recently the lease was granted.

Secondly, the provision only says that Rory is deemed to be a grantee of the original lease. It does not say that the burdens are deemed to have been part of

---

1 Title Conditions (Scotland) Act 2003, s 4(2)(b) is declaratory of the common law in relation to real burdens.
2 The subject is complex. See further D J Cusine and R R M Paisley *Servitudes and Rights of Way* (1998) paras 1.18, 2.12; W M Gordon *Scottish Land Law* (2nd edn, 1999) para 24-10.
3 See also on this provision K G C Reid *The Law of Property in Scotland* (1996) para 352.

that lease. So whilst one must wrestle with the intriguing consequences of Rory's being deemed alive in 1787, one of those consequences is *not* that the burdens were part of that lease, unless one adds words to the statute.

Thirdly, even if the provision had said that the burdens are deemed part of the original lease, then that would lead to the strange result that the lease would be deemed to have contained the burdens *from the start* – ever since 1787. The consequences are hard to contemplate.

Fourthly, even if the provision had said that the burdens are deemed part of the original lease, the effect would be not that *Margaret* could enforce but that the *landlord* could enforce, a most odd outcome. Alternatively, there might be an argument that Margaret could enforce by a sort of *jus quaesitum tertio*, on analogy with the parallel rules for co-feuars as set forth in *Hislop v MacRitchie's Trustees*.[1] But this is very speculative.[2]

Fifthly, even if the provision had said that the burdens are deemed part of the original lease, the effect would be that the burdens would bind Margaret's property as well as Rory's.

The conveyancing statute book contains few stranger provisions. What should it be understood as meaning? Indeed, can it really be understood as meaning anything at all? We offer no concluded view. Statutory provisions should be interpreted in a non-destructive manner. If some sort of good sense can be retrieved, retrieved it should be. But some statutory provisions are beyond the help of even the most benignant construction, and must be reluctantly and politely passed over as meaningless. The provision now under consideration must come near that point, and may cross over it.

The provision has now, for the first time, attracted judicial consideration: see *Griffiths v The Keeper of the Registers of Scotland*.[3] Two adjacent properties in Wishaw, No 75 and No 77 Kirk Road, were granted on two separate long leases in 1921. Both leases were eventually recorded in the Register of Sasines. In 1956 an assignation of No 77 purported to grant over No 77 a servitude right of way in favour of No 75.[4] This assignation was recorded. In due course both leases entered the Land Register, and the servitude was inserted on both title sheets, as a pertinent for No 75 and as a burden for No 77. Eventually the leaseholder for No 77 challenged the validity of the servitude and sought to have the Register rectified so that all reference to it would be deleted from both title sheets.

The Lands Tribunal had to consider two matters. First, had the servitude been validly constituted in 1956, before the leases were transferred to the Land Register? If so, that would be the end of the question. If not, then the Register was

---

1 *Hislop v MacRitchie's Trustees* (1881) 8 R (HL) 95.
2 Scottish Law Commission *Discussion Paper on Conversion of Long Leases* (Scot Law Com DP No 112, 2001) para 3.46.
3 *Griffiths v The Keeper of the Registers of Scotland* (20 December 2002, unreported), Lands Tribunal. The Tribunal comprised Lord McGhie and R F Durman FRICS.
4 Thus in *Griffiths* there was no break-off, unlike the Margaret/Rory example.

presumptively inaccurate,[1] and the consequences of that inaccuracy would have to be determined. The Tribunal answered the first question in the negative.[2]

If the 1956 grant was valid, it could be so only by virtue of the retrospective effect of s 3 of the Law Reform (Miscellaneous Provisions) (Scotland) Act 1985. The result would have been a quasi-servitude, binding the lease of No 77.[3] The Tribunal rejected this argument, apparently because it considered that s 3 could validate quasi-real burdens but not quasi-servitudes. The Tribunal discussion of s 3 is valuable but has few definite conclusions, though the Tribunal does observe, in carefully chosen language, that 'if it [s 3] is to receive effect, some creative inference as to the intention of the draftsman will be required'.[4]

Given the unclear state of the law, what can the conveyancer do? There seems to be no satisfactory answer, other than to involve the landlord/s, which may not be feasible. But it is possible that the difficulty is confined to quasi-servitudes, and that quasi-real burdens will be found to come within s 3 of the 1985 Act.

Agricultural Holdings (Scotland) Act 2003 (asp 11)

In this series we do not seek to cover agricultural tenancies. However, some mention of this important statute seems appropriate.[5]

Until 2003 the law was contained in the Agricultural Holdings (Scotland) Act 1991. Under that Act (and its predecessor, the Agricultural Holdings (Scotland) Act 1949) agricultural tenancies were virtually perpetual, regardless of what the parties may have agreed. This fact inevitably meant that owners of agricultural land were not prepared to let it out. However, a way of circumventing the 1991 Act was developed, whereby the farm was let to a partnership, whose partners were (1) the owner, as sleeping partner, and (2) the farmer, as managing partner. The owner could dissolve the partnership and thus terminate the lease. In practice limited partnerships were used, under the Limited Partnership Act 1907, since these shield the sleeping partner from liability to third parties. The validity of such arrangements was upheld in *MacFarlane v Falfield Investments Ltd.*[6]

It was felt that the law was too rigid, and should be reformed so as to make it possible for owners to grant leases that would not be perpetual. This reform is

---

1 But what about prescription? Certain facts are unclear, including whether the servitude had been actively used since 1956. If it had been so used, any defect in its constitution could have been cured by prescription. But that is so only if the two properties were separately owned (ie the two plots had different landlords), since *res sua nemini servit*. Whether they were separately owned was not established in the case, any more than whether the servitude had been in actual use. We do not know why these factual issues were left indeterminate. Prescription seems not to have been pled.

2 So the second question had to be dealt with: see pp 88–91 below.

3 Though apparently not in favour of No 75. See above.

4 *Griffiths v The Keeper of the Registers of Scotland* (20 December 2002, unreported), page 13 of the transcript. The word 'if' perhaps indicates an understandable doubt as to whether the section can receive effect.

5 For a discussion, see articles by Alasdair Fox in (2003) 48 *Journal of the Law Society of Scotland* May/58 and Dec/55.

6 *MacFarlane v Falfield Investments Ltd* 1998 SLT 145.

parallel to the reform that happened to residential tenancies in the 1980s. Just like that reform, the 2003 Act is not so radical as to allow freedom of contract. But it creates two new types of agricultural tenancy which the parties may choose, and these two new types are not perpetual.

First, there is the 'short limited duration tenancy'. This is for a *maximum* period of five years. Then there is the 'limited duration tenancy' which is for a *minimum* period of 15 years. A short limited duration tenancy is non-assignable, but a limited duration tenancy is assignable with the landlord's consent, which consent is not to be withheld unreasonably. In both types of lease irritancy clauses are valid, subject to certain qualifications. Rights of succession on death are regulated.[1]

These measures were relatively uncontroversial. Not so the right-to-buy provisions or the provisions applying to tenancies to limited partnerships.

The right to buy is in Part 2 of the Agricultural Holdings (Scotland) Act 2003. It is a pre-emptive right, meaning that it applies only on sale. The tenant must have sent to the Keeper a 'notice of interest'. The Keeper registers this in the Register of Community Interests in Land, established under the Land Reform (Scotland) Act 2003 (asp 2). If the owner (or a heritable creditor) wishes to sell, he must send a 'notice of proposal to transfer land' to the tenant and also register it in the Register. If the tenant wishes to buy he must respond with a notice. The price, if not agreed, is fixed by valuation. The basis of valuation is set out in s 34, and is, roughly speaking, what the market value would be taking into account the existence of the tenancy.

Section 72 of the Agricultural Holdings (Scotland) Act 2003 undermines the system of leases to limited partnerships by providing that if the partnership is dissolved the effect is simply to make the general partner (ie the farmer) the tenant. Thus if the tenant is a limited partnership, then 'any general partner [ie the farmer, in practice] may exercise or enforce any right of a tenant conferred by virtue of Part 2 of this Act [ie the right-to-buy provisions] as if the partner were the tenant'. It is understood that some owners are considering challenging the retrospective effect of s 72 as a breach of human rights.

Finally, where there is a lease subject to the 1991 Act or a limited duration tenancy, the 2003 Act has certain provisions allowing non-agricultural use of the land.[2]

Most of the Act is in force, the bulk of it as from 27 November 2003,[3] but Part 2 (right to buy) is not yet in force.[4]

---

1 Agricultural Holdings (Scotland) Act 2003, ss 20–22.
2 See AH(S)A 2003, Part 3.
3 Agricultural Holdings (Scotland) Act 2003 (Commencement No 1) Order 2003, SSI 2003/248; Agricultural Holdings (Scotland) Act 2003 (Commencement No 2) Order 2003, SSI 2003/305; Agricultural Holdings (Scotland) Act 2003 (Commencement No 3, Transitional and Savings Provisions) Order 2003, SSI 2003/548. See also the Agricultural Holdings (Relevant Date and Relevant Period) (Scotland) Order 2003, SSI 2003/294, and the Agricultural Holdings (Consequential Amendments) (Scotland) Order 2003, SSI 2003/583.
4 Strictly speaking, certain provisions of AH(S)A 2003, Part 2, are in force, but the right to buy is not yet in force.

Servitudes and rights of way

Prescriptive acquisition: is possession enough?

Webster v Chadburn[1] is an illuminating, but perhaps also a worrying, case on the acquisition of servitudes by prescription. The facts were unremarkable. Two cottages bordered a public road and could be reached from that road on foot. On another boundary there was a private road. By demolishing part of the fence separating the cottage garden from the private road, the cottages could be reached by car. Not surprisingly, this route came into standard usage and continued, openly, peaceably and without judicial interruption, for over 20 years. The road owner complained occasionally but ineffectually. From time to time he wrote letters without, usually, receiving any reply. On one occasion he pinned a note to the door of each cottage pointing out that he had seen a car parked on various occasions, that the car had obviously obtained access by means of the gap in the fence, and that the fence should be repaired. But matters continued as before.

Was there a servitude by prescription? The opinion of the sheriff principal,[2] at the end of a carefully reasoned judgment, was negative. True, there had been sufficient possession. For the purposes of prescription the possession must be 'as of right'. In the present case there was no evidence that this was so. No right had been conceded by the road owner. Further:[3]

> there is no finding as to the state of mind of any of those persons who drove their cars across the estate drive to the cottages between 1972 and 1994. Thus it is not known, for example, if any of them supposed, or had any reason to suppose, that he or she had any right to take access to the cottages in this way. When each of them first came on the scene he or she would have seen the gap in the fence and, no doubt, indications that cars had previously been driven through it to the cottages. Many of them were I dare say also told by previous occupants that they could drive through the gap to the cottages, and they would have found out soon enough that no objection was being made to their doing so. But there is nothing here beyond the fact of long continued use to support the view that, individually or collectively, these persons were asserting a right . . . as opposed to being permitted to do so by the proprietors of the estate.

It is true that when, after the 20-year period had elapsed, the owner of the cottages came to sell he included in the disposition

> a heritable and irredeemable servitude right of access for pedestrian and vehicular purposes over the area shown coloured pink on the plan annexed and subscribed as relative hereto.

---

1 *Webster v Chadburn* 2003 GWD 18-562.
2 Sir Stephen Young QC.
3 2003 GWD 18-562 at para [34].

But these words were less promising than at first they seemed, for the area coloured pink actually lay *within* the boundaries of the plot being disponed.

As the sheriff principal's opinion shows, there is a close relationship between possession 'as of right' and permission (or its absence) by the owner. Admittedly, the former looks to the actions of the putative benefited owner and the latter to the actions of the putative burdened; but the latter more or less determines the proper interpretation of the former. Three situations may be identified:

(1)   the burdened owner consents to the possession, expressly or implicitly;

(2)   the burdened owner does not consent to the possession (but does not succeed in preventing it);

(3)   the burdened owner does and says nothing, so that his intentions are unclear.

In the *first* situation (consent), no servitude can be established. Possession is attributable to permission and not to the assertion of a right; and permission, once given, can also be withdrawn. A prudent landowner wishing to prevent servitudes will make his consent clear, whether by notice or otherwise.[1] But consent can be established by implication as well as by express act, for otherwise the friendly tolerance of a neighbour could ripen into a hostile right.[2]

In the *third* situation (inactivity), the result appears to be the opposite. There is neither permission nor opposition; and a person who possesses for 20 years in the face of such indifference will, in general, be entitled to the servitude.[3]

Webster v Chadburn, however, was concerned with the *second* situation. The road owner made plain that he did not consent, but he took no active steps to stop the use. It might be thought that, from the standpoint of the putative benefited proprietor, this is an even stronger case than (3). In (3) the burdened proprietor's views are uncertain. In (2) they are clear: no permission has been given, and any exercise of possession, not being by permission, must necessarily be in assertion of a right.

The sheriff principal's view was different, however. No right had been conceded by the road owner. It was therefore for the cottage owner to show possession as of right. There were various ways in which this could be done. One would to demonstrate a (mistaken) belief that that the servitude already existed. Another would be for the cottage owner to make clear to the road owner that he was asserting a right. Neither was established. Indeed as to the latter the sheriff principal noted the failure of the cottage owner to respond to communications

---

1   *R (Beresford) v Sunderland City Council* [2003] 3 WLR 1306 at para [59] per Lord Rodger.

2   *McGregor v Crieff Co-operative Society Ltd* 1915 SC (HL) 93 at 107–08 per Lord Sumner.

3   D J Cusine and R R M Paisley *Servitudes and Rights of Way* (1998) pp 349–50. It is possible, however, that this situation too is affected by the reasoning in *Webster v Chadburn* 2003 GWD 18-562. On the other hand, counsel for the road owner 'accepted that, where there had been no indication of the position of the owner of the would-be servient tenement, so that there was nothing for the court to go on but the fact of use, then the volume of possession might in certain circumstances drive the court to the conclusion that this possession had been adverse and as of right': see para [30].

from the road owner by asserting a right to use it.[1] It followed, therefore, that possession was not as of right, and that no servitude had been established.

If this is the law, it significantly cuts down the circumstances in which a prescriptive servitude can be established. Mere possession is not enough. Instead there is something like a duty of good faith. The putative benefited owner must either be ignorant (ie must believe that he already has the right) or honest (ie must make clear to the other owner that he hopes to acquire the right by usage).[2] But this seems to go well beyond the existing authorities. Good faith is not part of our law of positive prescription, whether for the acquisition servitudes or for the acquisition of ownership. It is commonplace for a person to use a road with, as it were, an eye to prescription. He knows the road is not his and that he has no right to be on it. Yet he carries on regardless. The decision in *Webster v Chadburn* seems to require him to make a clean breast of matters to the road owner. It is unlikely that this would happen in practice. But it is unlikely, too, that this is really the law. It is not the rule for the prescriptive acquisition of public rights of way,[3] and the rules are the same for both cases.[4]

As it happens, the issue of possession as of right was also considered in 2003 by the House of Lords in an English appeal, *R (Beresford) v Sunderland City Council*.[5] This concerned the right of local inhabitants to register land as a village green, but the relevant test for possession, it was accepted, was the same as for the prescriptive acquisition of public rights of way (and therefore of servitudes). The villagers were held to have possessed as of right without any inquiry into their state of mind of the kind envisaged by the sheriff principal in *Webster*. And in the course of his speech Lord Bingham disposed of the idea that to possess as of right it is necessary to believe that one has the right in the first place:[6]

> In this context it is plain that 'as of right' does not require that the inhabitants should have a legal right since in this, as in other cases of prescription, the question is whether a party who lacks a legal right has acquired one by use for a stipulated period. It is also plain that 'as of right' does not require that the inhabitants should believe themselves to have a legal right.

This, of course, is a decision on English law. But in the same case Lord Rodger had this to say:[7]

> In a memorable passage in *Napier's Trustees v Morrison*[8] dealing with a public right of way, Lord Cockburn deprecated the citation in the Court of Session of authorities

---

1 *Webster v Chadburn* 2003 GWD 18-562 at paras [35], [36].
2 Or perhaps – it is not clear from the judgment – simply have a verifiable, though uncommunicated, intention to acquire the right.
3 *Cumbernauld and Kilsyth District Council v Dollar Land (Cumbernauld) Ltd* 1993 SC (HL) 44.
4 Prescription and Limitation (Scotland) Act 1973, s 3.
5 *R (Beresford) v Sunderland City Council* [2003] 3 WLR 1306.
6 [2003] 3 WLR 1306 at para [3].
7 [2003] 3 WLR 1306 at para [64].
8 *Napier's Trustees v Morrison* (1851) 13 D 1404 at 1409.

from England. He really wished, he said – taking a swipe at a future Lord President among others – that Scottish counsel and judges 'could imitate the example set us by the counsel and the judges of that kingdom, who decide their causes by their own rules and customs, without exposing themselves by referring to foreign systems, the very language of which they do not comprehend'. Times change: in the course of the hearing of this appeal well-informed counsel on both sides referred your Lordships to a number of Scottish authorities on the acquisition of servitudes and public rights of way ... While exercising all due caution, and at the risk of disturbing the shade of Lord Cockburn, I believe that the Scottish authorities can provide some assistance in this case, at least by way of confirming the conclusion that I have already reached.

The same is true the other way around. English law, indeed, is quite often a useful quarry in this area of law in a way that it is not in property law generally. The point is illustrated in the next case.

Parking

Only certain types of right can be created as servitudes. There is, in other words, a virtual fixed list – a *numerus clausus* – of servitudes. It is true that the courts have often said that the list can be added to, but what the courts say and what they do are, in this field, not the same. The most recent servitude, bleaching, is now more than 200 years old. Though the list is, for most practical purposes, fixed, some flexibility is created by the fact that its content is opaque. We know that the list is fixed, but we do not know exactly what is on it.

One of the most difficult, and practically important, examples is parking. After an exhaustive examination of this topic, running to nine pages, Sheriff Cusine and Professor Paisley write:[1]

> Our conclusion is that these authorities are not particularly helpful in that in none of them was the issue directly in point, and therefore no adviser can say with confidence that a right to park will ever be recognised. However, in our opinion there are compelling arguments for its recognition in some instances.

After a long wait,[2] there is now a case where the issue of parking was, indeed, 'directly in point': *Moncreiffe v Jamieson*.[3]

The dispute was between neighbours in Sandsound in Shetland. The pursuers had a number of craves, including declarator, interdict and damages. Property owned by the pursuers faced the sea and could be reached from the landward side only by a private road[4] running through the third defenders' land. At one time both properties had belonged to the same person, but the pursuers'

---

1 D J Cusine and R R M Paisley *Servitudes and Rights of Way* (1998) p 188.
2 See, however, *Davidson v Wiseman* 2001 GWD 9-317, discussed in *Conveyancing 2001* pp 72–3.
3 *Moncrieffe v Jamieson* (2003, unreported), Lerwick Sheriff Court.
4 In fact it was discovered at the time of the litigation that the private road to some extent followed the route of a derelict public road, as to which there was assumed to be a public right. But this finding is not material for present purposes.

property was broken off by a disposition in 1973. This conferred 'a right of access from the branch public road through Sandsound'. There could be no dispute, therefore, as to the pursuers' right to use the road itself. But because of the steep fall in the land there could be no question of taking a car on to their own property. Further, the access road was too narrow for a vehicle to turn. Accordingly, the pursuers' practice was to use part of the defenders' land to turn and to park. The pursuers added hardstanding. Matters proceeded amicably until 1998 when the defenders decided to build a wall taking in most of the turning area. Works were begun, to the prejudice of the pursuers. The central issue was whether the pursuers had a servitude of parking.

The sheriff[1] held that a right of parking existed. The argument ran thus. (1) There was a servitude of way. (2) Servitudes of way can include ancillary rights, such as the right to stop for the purposes of loading and unloading. (3) In practical terms there may often be little difference between unloading and parking. 'One could, no doubt, park for less than five minutes and take many hours to load or unload a pantechnicon – though perhaps the latter operations would be unlikely to take place overnight.' (4) The physical circumstances were such that a proper use of the servitude of way almost necessarily required a right of parking. Otherwise the pursuers would have to park some distance, and height, away, on the main road.[2] (5) Accordingly, in creating a servitude of way in 1993 the granters must be taken to have included, by implication, a right of parking.

The argument that the law might not recognise such a servitude was, apparently, not much pressed and was brushed aside by the sheriff as being 'greatly overstated':

> It is obvious that a servitude of vehicle parking is a prime candidate for recognition and our law is flexible enough to allow that to happen. It is not a large step to recognise a right to park as ancillary to a right of access. Other jurisdictions have done so.

The other jurisdictions include England and Wales,[3] a source worth consulting in the case of the law of servitudes:

> As the origins of both Scottish servitudes and English easements jointly lie in Roman law and as counsel for the Pursuers said, though English land law is largely very different from ours, in the matter of servitudes and easements at least there is a considerable confluence.

The decision is not authority for the existence of a servitude of parking, as such. Rather, the right which the sheriff found to exist was ancillary to an

---

1 Sheriff Colin Mackenzie.
2 This is an argument made forcibly in D J Cusine and R R M Paisley *Servitudes and Rights of Way* (1998) para 3.51.
3 *Blenheim Estates Ltd v Ladbroke Retail Parks Ltd* [1992] 1 WLR 1278 at 1285-8, affd [1994] 1 WLR 31. Like all servitudes, however, the right must not be so extensive as to negate ownership: see eg *Batchelor v Marlow* (2001) 82 P & CR 459.

established servitude, namely a servitude of way. In *obiter* remarks, however, the sheriff went further. Had he not identified a right of parking as ancillary to a right of way he would, he said, have been prepared to recognise it as a servitude in his own right, constituted, on the present facts, either by implied grant or by acquiescence.[1] But it was unnecessary to do so.

Taken as a whole, the decision is an important step towards the recognition of parking as a servitude. A definitive decision – a decision by the Court of Session on a freestanding right of parking – is, however, still awaited.

As well as being willing to recognise a servitude of parking, the sheriff was also willing, in principle, to recognise as a servitude a right to store fuel and building material. But such a right was clearly not ancillary to a right of way, and the facts did not sufficiently establish a freestanding servitude, whether by implied grant or by acquiescence.

The position just described is changed in important ways by the Title Conditions (Scotland) Act 2003 when it comes fully into force on 28 November 2004. The fixed list is abandoned in respect of servitudes created by writing and registration.[2] As long as a right is servitude-like and of moderate dimensions, it does not matter that it has not been previously recognised by the law. Thus in the future there will be no difficulty in creating freestanding rights of parking. But the move away from a fixed list does not apply to servitudes created in other ways – by implied grant, for example, or by prescription. Nor is the change retrospective. Rights expressly created in existing titles will continue to be judged by the present law – whatever that law turns out to be.

Verges and public roads

For the purposes of the Roads (Scotland) 1984, a road includes its verge.[3] A verge may be indeterminate. Yet it may be important to know where the verge ends and the adjoining land begins. Since the verge is part of the road it demarcates rights of use, and may demarcate ownership. The roads authority can use the verge for road signs, bus shelters, sound barriers and the like,[4] and those who own adjacent land can use the verge to get to and from the road. If the roads authority owns land beyond the verge, then it has a ransom strip separating the road from neighbouring land.[5]

Until recently there was little authority as to what constitutes a verge. The issued is addressed in *David Runciman & Sons v Scottish Borders Council*.[6] The case concerned the D74/6 at Chirnside in the Borders. At the relevant point the road had a grass verge culminating in a beech hedge. The petitioners owned the land

---

1 The right had not been exercised for long enough to allow prescription to run.
2 Title Conditions (Scotland) Act 2003, s 76. See further p 130.
3 Roads (Scotland) Act 1984, s 151(1).
4 *David Runciman & Sons v Scottish Borders Council* 2003 SLT 1405 at para [6] per Lord Drummond Young.
5 *Elmford Ltd v City of Glasgow Council (No 2)* 2001 SC 267, discussed in *Conveyancing 2000* pp 51–2.
6 *David Runciman & Sons v Scottish Borders Council* 2003 SLT 1405.

on either side. They erected a post-and-wire fence on the road side of the hedge. Their purpose, it appears, was to stake out their ownership in order to resist a possible residential development which could not be built without new passing places. Scottish Borders Council ordered the removal of the fence.[1] The order was challenged by the petitioners. The result turned on the precise boundary of the verge. If the verge ended before the fence began, the petitioners were within their rights. If, however, the verge included the site of the fence, the Council were entitled to require its removal.

In many cases, the Lord Ordinary (Drummond Young) said, it will be easy to determine the extent of a verge:[2]

[T]he position is reasonably straightforward where a road is bounded by an established wall or fence or by a building. In such cases the boundary of the verge will normally be taken as the roadward face of the wall, fence or building . . .[3] In such cases there exists an obvious physical barrier that stretches upwards from the ground and is obviously designed to separate the road and its verge from the property beyond. At the other extreme are cases where there is no barrier of any sort, and the road extends into un-enclosed fields, rough grazing or moorland; in the absence of a barrier the verge must clearly be reasonable in extent, and what is reasonable will depend on function rather than any physical barrier on the ground.[4]

In the case of a hedge, however, the position is less certain. The Council argued that the boundary was mid-line of the hedge, determined by reference to the trunks. The petitioners argued for the roadward face of the branches; and, given that branches both grow and are pruned, this was to be measured by reference to 'the mean annual greatest growth'. Both alternatives were rejected by the court as being too uncertain – a criticism directed particularly at the second. Instead:[5]

The boundary must lie along the roadward side of the trunks of the shrubs or trees that make up the hedge. That provides a reasonably clear and definite boundary; in many respects it is similar to the boundary provided by a post and wire fence. It is also a boundary that can be ascertained at ground level with reasonable clarity.

On that basis the fence was on the 'wrong' side of the hedge, and so was on the verge. Accordingly the Council could require its removal.

Brief mention may be made of three other matters. First, the definition of 'road'

1 Under the Roads (Scotland) Act 1984, s 87(1).
2 2003 SLT 1405 at para [5].
3 This statement relies on *County Council of Perth and Kinross v Magistrates of Crieff* 1933 SC 751 at 761 per Lord Murray.
4 Whilst we would not dissent, we would observe that beneath these rules lurk considerable difficulties, both practical and theoretical. Does a frontager who plants a hedge thereby permanently define the verge? If so, does that power exist not only if he happens to plant it well back from the road but also when he plants it hard up against the road? What if a frontager moves a long-standing fence back half a metre away from the road? Would that widen the verge? Does it make a difference how long the hedge or fence has been there?
5 *David Runciman & Sons v Scottish Borders Council* 2003 SLT 1405 at para [5].

in the Roads (Scotland) Act 1984 is 'any way . . . over which there is a public right of passage'.[1] The petitioners argued that no passage could in practice be taken close to the hedge because of the branches, and therefore the road (and verge) must be roadward of the branches. The court disagreed:[2]

> It is true that a public right of passage is necessary if a road is to fall within the statutory definition. It does not follow, however, that it is necessary that passage should be possible, or even practicable, over every part of the area of such a road.

Secondly, the court rejected as unimportant the evidence that it was the petitioners and not the Council who had in practice maintained the grass area and hedge. That 'might be of evidential value in a doubtful case, but that is all'.[3]

Finally, since one effect of the decision was to give roads authorities the right to cut back hedges, at least on the roadward side[4] – and since such a hedge was nonetheless the property of the neighbouring landowners – the Lord Ordinary offered some thoughts on the extent of such a right:[5]

> [T]he roads authority are under an obligation to keep any interference with the hedge to the minimum that is required to enable them to perform their functions. If interference with the hedge is necessary, I consider that the roads authority must keep in mind that the hedge acts not merely as a boundary but also as a means of fencing a field or garden; thus the authority must ensure that fencing is maintained. I further consider that the roads authority must take into consideration that a fence may act as a windbreak or to stop soil erosion, and may also serve an important aesthetic purpose. If follows that if, for example, a road sign or barrier is sited in an area overhung by a hedge, the necessary excavations should do as little damage as possible to the roots of the hedge, and damage to the branches should be kept to a minimum.

Verges and servitudes

A verge is part of a public road and so can, in principle, be used for access. The rule for servitudes is different. The general principle was set out in *Stansfield v Findlay*:[6]

> We did not find support in any of the authorities cited to us for the view that, as a matter of law, the track over which access is to be provided must be construed as including its 'verges' . . . We accept that there may be cases in which it can be inferred that a right of way which passes between fenced enclosures extends to the full width between the fences and is not limited to a worn or metalled track lying within that area. That may, for example, be the case with former drove roads. Each case depends on its own facts.

---

1 Roads (Scotland) Act 1984, s 151(1).
2 *David Runciman & Sons v Scottish Borders Council* 2003 SLT 1405 at para [9].
3 2003 SLT 1405 at para [12].
4 R(S)A 1984, s 91.
5 2003 SLT 1405 at para [8].
6 *Stansfield v Findlay* 1998 SLT 784 at 787L–788B per Lord Macfadyen.

As the court indicated, sometimes a verge is included within a servitude.[1] More usually, however, it is not. The new case of *Thomas v Allan*[2] is an example of the usual rule. The servitude there was described as 'a right of access ... by the existing service road'. It was accepted by both sides that this did not by itself extend to the verges (which the defenders had obstructed). The only question was whether that original servitude had been innovated on by a later deed so as to include the verges. As a matter of construction, it was held that no such innovation had incurred.[3]

Standard securities

Cautionary wives

In 1997 there were two House of Lords decisions on Scots law that made a great stir. In both a unanimous Court of Session decision was reversed. In both the reversal was controversial.[4] Both cases recast the law in an English mould. Both cases have proved unpopular with the Scottish judiciary, which has taken every opportunity to limit their scope. One case was *Sharp v Thomson*.[5] The other was *Smith v Bank of Scotland*, the 'cautionary wives' case.[6] Case law has been more prolific on *Smith* than on *Sharp*,[7] and accordingly cautionary wives have featured regularly in these updates.[8] 2003 has brought more decisions. *Smith* is now near to death by a thousand cuts, and indeed in 2003 we even find the Lord Justice Clerk saying that *Smith*, on its own facts, was not a case subject to the *Smith* doctrine. The actual success rate of the *Smith* doctrine in reported cases continues to be 0%.

What is the *Smith* doctrine? Before *Smith*, if the principal obligant induced a cautioner to sign by undue influence or misrepresentation, that did not constitute a defence for the cautioner against the creditor, assuming, of course, that the creditor was in good faith. But in *Smith* the House of Lords said that in certain circumstances the creditor would cease to be in good faith unless positively

---

1 An example is *Wimpey Homes Holdings Ltd v Collins* 1999 SLT (Sh Ct) 16, although there may be a question whether, after *Stansfield v Findlay* 1998 SLT 784, *Wimpey* is still good law.

2 *Thomas v Allan* 2004 GWD 1-15.

3 In the construction of the later deed the court, properly, resisted the argument that the wording should be read *civiliter*. See 2004 GWD 1-15 at para [14]. *Civiliter* is a principle of use and not of interpretation.

4 Much of the literature on the *Smith* doctrine is mentioned in Sandra Eden's valuable article, 'Cautionary Tales' (2003) 7 *Edinburgh Law Review* 107.

5 *Sharp v Thompson* 1997 SC (HL) 66.

6 *Smith v Bank of Scotland* 1997 SC (HL) 111. The *Smith* doctrine is nominally gender-neutral but substantively gendered.

7 Though, on *Sharp*, see now *Burnett's Trustee v Grainger* 2004 GWD 9-211, which greatly restricts its scope.

8 *Conveyancing 1999* pp 54–6; *Conveyancing 2000* pp 86–91; *Conveyancing 2001* pp 92–6; *Conveyancing 2002* pp 59–63.

satisfied that the cautioner's signature had been fairly obtained. These circumstances were, in the words of Lord Clyde:[1]

> such as to lead a reasonable man to believe that owing to the personal relationship between the debtor and the proposed cautioner, the latter's consent may not be fully informed or freely given.

How might the creditor be positively satisfied that the consent was a genuine one? Lord Clyde again:[2]

> All that is required of him [ie the creditor] is that he should take reasonable steps to secure that in relation to the proposed contract he acts throughout in good faith. So far as the substance of those steps is concerned it seems to me that it would be sufficient for the creditor to warn the potential cautioner of the consequences of entering into the proposed cautionary obligation and to advise him or her to take independent advice.

That is the doctrine in outline. But evidently there was scope for dispute about the details. One has been whether the wife, in seeking to escape, needs to prove that her consent was unfairly obtained, or whether it is sufficient to show merely that the creditor had not taken the sort of steps contemplated by Lord Clyde. The case law has suggested that the former is necessary. A second area of dispute has been whether the creditor's good faith is protected if the wife has had legal advice (or even if the creditor reasonably believes that she has had legal advice), or whether the creditor needs to be sure that the legal advice was sufficient. Here the case law has indicated that the lower standard is the applicable one. A third area of dispute has been as to when the higher level of duty comes into play. A fourth, an overarching issue, has been whether *Smith* simply introduced English law as such, so that English authorities will be more or less decisive in Scotland, or whether Scots law is free to find its own way. All these issues have been litigated again in 2003.

First, *Royal Bank of Scotland plc v Wilson*.[3] Francis Wilson and John Wilson were brothers. Francis was married to Annette. John was married to Norma. In 1991 Francis and Annette borrowed from the Royal Bank of Scotland plc (RBS) to buy a house. About the same time John and Norma borrowed from RBS to build a conservatory. The loans were secured on their respective houses at 98 and 100 Dalum Grove, Loanhead, Midlothian, each of which was co-owned by the respective spouses.

The brothers were in partnership together, and indeed they had two firms, F J Wilson Associates and Wilson Brothers. After the two loans just mentioned were taken out, these firms also borrowed from the same bank, RBS. Both firms

---

1 *Smith v Bank of Scotland* 1997 SC (HL) 111 at 121.
2 1997 SC (HL) 111 at 122.
3 *Royal Bank of Scotland plc v Wilson* 2003 SC 544, 2003 SLT 910, 2003 SCLR 716. For discussion see: Swinton (2003) 71 *Scottish Law Gazette* 113; Thomson (2003) 71 *Scottish Law Gazette* 158; Stirling (2003) 53/54 *Greens Civil Practice Bulletin* 7.

eventually defaulted. The bank then called on the partners to pay, but the partners defaulted too. When the bank was unable to recover the partnership loans, it sought to enforce the two standard securities.

Both standard securities provided:

> We ... and ... spouses ... (hereinafter referred to as 'the Obligant') hereby undertake to pay to The Royal Bank of Scotland plc (hereinafter referred to as 'the Bank', which expression includes its successors and assignees whomsoever) on demand all sums of principal, interest and charges which are now and which may at any time hereafter become due to the Bank by the Obligant whether solely or jointly with any other person, corporation, firm or other body and whether as principal or surety; declaring that ... in the event of the foregoing personal obligation being granted by more than one person the expression 'the Obligant' means all such persons together and/or any one or more of them; and in all cases the obligations hereby undertaken by the Obligant shall bind all person(s) included in the expression 'the Obligant' and his, her or their executors and representatives whomsoever all jointly and severally without the necessity of discussing them in their order.[1]

This is a thicket of words, whose suitability in a consumer transaction, in terms both of form and substance, may be questioned. That it means that each granter is liable without limit for all debts, including future debts, due by the other granter is hardly obvious at first reading.[2] But that indeed is its meaning. 'A lender', it has been said, 'who makes advances to B without the consent of A on the basis of an earlier security, entered into by A and B for another purpose entirely, is at least engaged in extremely questionable practice.'[3] The issue has now come before the courts twice, once in the present case and the other, a year or two back, in *Ahmed v Clydesdale Bank*.[4] In neither case was the wife successful, but it may be wondered whether the battle on this issue is yet over. Untried arguments may exist. For instance there might be an argument based on the Unfair Terms in Consumer Contracts Regulations 1999, SI 1999/2083.

In *Wilson* the action was an application under s 24 of the Conveyancing and Feudal Reform (Scotland) Act 1970 for warrant to sell. The wives resisted the application on the basis of the *Smith* doctrine.[5] They pled that they had been the victim of misrepresentations by their husbands to the effect that the securities related purely to the house purchase (in one case) or house extension (in the other), and that had it not been for this misrepresentation they would never have signed. There were also averments that the bank manager had been guilty of misrepresentation. These various alleged misrepresentations, however, were

---

1 The conservatism of legal drafting is striking. The final words, excluding the *beneficium discussionis*, have been unnecessary since the Mercantile Law Amendment (Scotland) Act 1856, which provided that the *beneficium* would henceforth exist only on an opt-in rather than an opt-out basis. (Like the rest of that Act, the reform was misconceived.)
2 Such debts are secured not only on the property: each spouse is also personally liable.
3 Eden (2003) 7 *Edinburgh Law Review* 107, 114.
4 *Ahmed v Clydesdale Bank* 2001 SLT 423. See *Conveyancing 2000* p 89.
5 There was also a plea that the husbands were not liable to pay the debts of the firms. The basis of that plea does not appear from the report and it is irrelevant for present purposes.

constituted by silence. The argument was that there existed an active duty to explain to the wives the precise meaning and effect of the deeds. The wives argued that the decision of the House of Lords in the English case of *Royal Bank of Scotland plc v Etridge (No 2)*[1] should be extended to Scots law.

The Second Division unanimously rejected these arguments. In the first place, the starting point is 'whether the husband has committed an actionable wrong against his wife'.[2] Mere silence was not misrepresentation. A husband is under no obligation to volunteer information. Since the husband had not 'committed an actionable wrong against his wife' the case did not get to first base. This approach is in line with earlier decisions, such as *Braithwaite v Royal Bank of Scotland*.[3]

In the second place, in the words of Lord Justice Clerk Gill:[4]

> these appeals fail on the ground that the second defenders did not incur the cautionary obligation gratuitously. In incurring a cautionary obligation in respect of her husband's future debts, each received the benefit of a co-extensive obligation on his part in respect of her own. In *Smith v Bank of Scotland* the discussion seems to have proceeded on the assumption that the wife incurred a cautionary obligation in respect of her husband's debts and got nothing in return. The Session Papers in *Smith v Bank of Scotland* show that the standard security was an all-sums security in similar terms to these, but this point was not taken in that case. In my view, it is a decisive point in the present cases.

In other words, *Smith* was not, on its facts, an example of the *Smith* doctrine.

The idea that the higher level of good faith on the part of the creditor does not arise unless the wife has acted 'gratuitously' has little prominence in the earlier cases. Its importance is considerable. 'A wife will normally have an interest, indirect but nonetheless significant, in the success of her husband's business', remarked Lord Gill.[5] In fact he seems not to have based his decision on this point, for there were other reasons why the deed was not gratuitous. But if it is accepted that the typical spousal guarantee is in substance not gratuitous, then the *Smith* doctrine is virtually dead.

In the third place, the standard securities had been prepared by solicitors. One firm acted for Francis and his wife and another for John and his wife. The wives claimed that they had received no advice from these firms as to the effect of the standard securities. This claim was held irrelevant. In the words of Lord Gill, 'if the cautioner, to the knowledge of the creditor, is represented in relation to the transaction by an independent solicitor, I cannot see why the creditor should have to verify the content and the quality of his advice.'[6] He added that 'the question is not what advice the cautioner received. It is whether the creditor was entitled to assume that the solicitor had given appropriate advice.'[7] This is in line

---

1 *Royal Bank of Scotland plc v Etridge (No 2)* [2002] 2 AC 773.
2 *Royal Bank of Scotland plc v Wilson* 2003 SC 544 at para [25].
3 *Braithwaite v Royal Bank of Scotland* 1999 SLT 25.
4 *Royal Bank of Scotland plc v Etridge (No 2)* [2002] 2 AC 773 at para [24].
5 *Royal Bank of Scotland plc v Wilson* 2003 SC 544 at para [32].
6 2003 SC 544 at para [31].
7 2003 SC 544 at para [36].

with previous decisions on the *Smith* doctrine. For instance, in *Forsyth v Royal Bank of Scotland*[1] it was held that if the wife has been advised by a solicitor then the bank is entitled to assume that she has been properly advised, while in *Clydesdale Bank plc v Black*[2] the Inner House took the view that *Royal Bank of Scotland v Etridge (No 2)* does not represent the law of Scotland.

Although *Wilson* is consistent with earlier case law, it should not be regarded as having been a foregone conclusion. There did exist the possibility that the court might have taken a radical, and much more English, approach. But to counsel's argument that no solicitor could properly allow a client to grant a deed in those terms, Lord Gill replied that:[3]

> It is not the solicitor's duty not to allow his client to enter into such a transaction. A wife will normally have an interest, indirect but nonetheless significant, in the success of her husband's business. Since the wife's decision may be influenced by many considerations, personal as well as financial, the solicitor must leave her to make up her own mind. The solicitor's duty is only to give the wife accurate advice as to the effect of the proposed transaction and as to the conflicts of interest that may exist between her and her husband. In my view, the requirement of good faith is adequately met if the creditor has no objective basis for thinking that the solicitor acting for the wife has been deficient in his professional responsibilities in these respects.

However, in one respect the court doubted *Clydesdale Bank plc v Black*. In that case the view was taken that the *Smith* doctrine applied only to guarantees and securities granted after the *Smith* case itself in 1997. The reason was that in *Smith* the House of Lords said quite openly that it was changing the law of Scotland, and that the Court of Session in *Smith* had decided the case correctly. Since the House of Lords was, in effect, legislating, the legislation presumptively had no retrospective effect. There is much to be said for that view, but in *Wilson* it was doubted.

In this area cases are plentiful, and *Wilson* has already been applied in the Outer House in two further cases, namely *Christie v Bank of Scotland*[4] and *Thomson v Royal Bank of Scotland*.[5]

In the first of these, Richard and Vivienne Christie were co-owners of Woodside Farm, Monkton. They were also the directors of a company, Busby Equitation Centre Ltd. In June 1992 the Christies signed a guarantee to the bank for the borrowings of the company. Later the same year they both granted a standard security to the bank for all sums due and to become due. Eventually the bank sought to enforce the guarantee and standard security. Mrs Christie responded by raising an action to reduce both deeds. The action was dismissed as irrelevant by temporary judge T G Coutts QC. The guarantee was not

---

1 *Forsyth v Royal Bank of Scotland* 2000 SLT 1295.
2 *Clydesdale Bank plc v Black* 2002 SLT 764. See *Conveyancing* 2002 p 60.
3 *Royal Bank of Scotland plc v Wilson* 2003 SC 544 at para [32].
4 *Christie v Bank of Scotland* 2003 GWD 29-803.
5 *Thomson v Royal Bank of Scotland* 2003 SCLR 964.

gratuitous since both spouses, as directors, had an interest in its affairs. 'Both husband and wife had a clear interest in the maintenance of the company and in any event the Personal Guarantee was not in order to relieve the husband of obligations but to share the consequences of obligations incurred or to be incurred by the company.'[1] With respect, the second part of this statement probably goes too far. The *Smith* doctrine would seem to apply, at least potentially, to any case where the wife guarantees the debts of her husband's business, even if that business is conducted as a separate entity, such as a company.[2] As for the standard security, the wife's challenge failed for the usual reason: the existence of legal advice.

Many of the cases have been dismissed on grounds of relevancy. *Thomson v Royal Bank of Scotland* is one that made it to proof.[3] The husband had a company, and the husband and wife granted a standard security for the company's debts. Unlike *Christie*, the wife had no connection with the company. The evidence was that the wife's signature had not been obtained by unfair means. Referring to *Wilson*, Lord Clarke commented that:[4]

> the opinions in that case ... have demonstrated the danger of falling ... into the trap of believing that the law of Scotland considers that there is anything even approaching an automatic presumption that a wife who grants a security over the matrimonial home, jointly owned with her husband, when that security is granted in respect of borrowings by a business in which the husband has an interest, has, if not separately advised, had an actionable wrong committed against her.

Lord Clarke went on to refer to 'the implicit trust (based on previous experience) that the wife has placed in her husband's judgment. It is not the function of the law ... to subvert such relationships of trust'.[5]

While not adding anything new, the decision offers valuable analysis of *Wilson* and it shows, yet again, that the Scottish courts are slow to apply the *Smith* doctrine in practice. A final point of interest is that there was uncertainty as to whether the solicitor who drew up the standard security, and who was acting for the bank and for the borrower (the company), was also acting for Mr and Mrs Thomson. This issue did not have to be resolved, but the point illustrates how easy it is for such matters to become unclear.

The lack of success of cautionary wives against banks must not distract attention from the duty of solicitors to give proper advice, especially when it is recalled that one of the reasons for that lack of success has been that banks are entitled to assume that proper advice has been given. If clients do sign a standard security of the *Wilson* sort, not only should its implications be explained, but it should perhaps be suggested that, if either spouse wishes in the future to borrow

---

1 *Christie v Bank of Scotland* 2003 GWD 29-803 at para [23].
2 See eg Eden (2003) 7 *Edinburgh Law Review* 107, 113.
3 *Thomson v Royal Bank of Scotland* 2003 SCLR 964. For the earlier stages of this case see *Conveyancing 2002* p 21.
4 2003 SCLR 964 at para [50].
5 2003 SCLR 964 at para [51].

money by himself or herself, the bank chosen should be a different bank, so as not to bring the other spouse in as an involuntary cautioner.

How common standard securities of the *Wilson* type are is unclear. Joint standard securities are often obscurely worded. It is normal for the same standard form to be used for sole borrowers and for joint borrowers. A random survey of some modern styles used by institutional lenders shows that most are similar to each other but not quite the same as the style used in *Wilson*.[1] Those we have looked at say that the deed covers not only (1) the loan but also (2) all debts in future owed to the lender by the borrower. Since 'borrower' has been defined as meaning 'Hamish McGlumfrey *and* Morag McGoist or McGlumfrey', it can be argued that only future debts owed by *both* are covered by the deed. Most (but not quite all) of the styles do, indeed, state that where there are joint borrowers, liability is joint and several. But that, it may be argued, only means that liability is joint and several *for the debts covered by the deed*. It does not say anything about which debts the deed covers. In other words, it is arguable that deeds of this sort do not have the same effect as a deed of the *Wilson* type. But we have not made a systematic study of styles, and in any case the argument just advanced may well not be conclusive.[2] So clients should be warned that even with deeds of this sort there may be a danger. Why banks choose styles whose effects are – to us at least – obscure we do not understand.

Once upon a time such problems seldom arose, for mortgage lending was provided by building societies and commercial lending by banks, so that when clients signed a standard security for a home loan the danger that one spouse might obtain commercial credit from the same lender was remote. But times have changed.

In 2003 both the Professional Practice Committee and the Conveyancing Committee of the Law Society of Scotland issued advice about spousal cases. The former advised that:[3]

> Solicitors should be mindful to advise fully joint obligants (husbands and wives) of the nature of an 'all sums due' security. In particular it should be drawn to their attention that additional loans for example in respect of one of the obligant's businesses, may give rise to further secured borrowings without the other obligant requiring to sign the documentation. In such circumstances there is also a conflict of interest between the joint obligants.

The precise meaning of this passage may be open to debate. It may refer only to standard securities where business borrowing by the husband is in contemplation.

---

1 We have looked at what we understand is the current standard style used by the RBS and it appears to be substantially the same as the one used in *Royal Bank of Scotland plc v Wilson* 2003 SC 544. In our random survey the only lender that used a style which appeared to be similar to that of the RBS was the Clydesdale Bank plc.
2 Moreover we have not undertaken a survey of each lender's 'mortgage conditions' which are typically incorporated by reference into each standard security. These could easily affect the position.
3 (2003) 48 *Journal of the Law Society of Scotland* Oct/47.

But it might refer, more widely, to any standard security that is so worded that the wife could become liable for loans made solely to the husband. In the latter case the implications for practice may be substantial, since conflict of interest means separate legal advice.

The Conveyancing Committee suggests a style of letter to be sent 'to a wife when she is granting standard security over the matrimonial home to secure a loan to her husband or his business.' Here is the style:[1]

Dear

This letter confirms the advice that [I] [we] gave you at our meeting [today] in respect of the proposals that your house known as [   ] (the Property) is to be mortgaged to [   ] (the Lender) to secure a loan from the Lender to [   ] (the Borrower).

The Lender requires that you are given this advice so that having signed the standard security (mortgage deed) [and related documents] you will not be able to claim afterwards that you are not legally bound by [it] [them].

1. The property is owned [in your sole name] [in the Borrower's sole name] [in the joint names of yourself and [   ]] and you [both] are required to sign [the standard security] [and related documents] in favour of the Lender.

2. Enclosed are copies of the standard security which you signed earlier today [and the mortgage conditions that are incorporated into it] [and related documents]. The following is a summary of the main provisions and implications, but does not cover everything.

3. The standard security is [initially] required to give the Lender security for a loan [of £   ] [a loan facility of up to £   ] to be provided to the Borrower. However, the mortgage will be on 'all sums due or to become due' terms and will also give the Lender security over the Property for:

    (1) any further loan or increased facility that the Borrower (individually or jointly with you or anyone else) may in future obtain from the Lender while the standard security remains in existence, even if this is done without your knowledge or consent;

    (2) any existing loans from the Lender to the Borrower (individually or jointly with you or anyone else), even if you do not know about them;

    (3) any existing or future loans that you yourself may obtain (individually or jointly with anyone else) from the Lender while the standard security remains in existence;

    (4) any sums owing to the Lender, at any time while the standard security remains in existence, by any other person or company if you or the Borrower has already given, or shall in future give, a guarantee for those sums to the Lender, and even if the Borrower has given or shall give such a guarantee without your knowledge and consent;

---

1 (2003) 48 *Journal of the Law Society of Scotland* Oct/38.

(5)   interest on all such sums as charged by the Lender;

(6)   [anything else];

According to the terms of the loan the Lender can demand repayment at [any time], [on fixed dates], [by instalments,] [set out repayment requirements].

4.   During the subsistence of the mortgage, [you] [the Borrower] must:

(1)   keep the Property insured in accordance with the Lender's requirements;

(2)   keep the Property in good repair;

(3)   not make any structural alterations or changes of use without the Lender's consent;

(4)   not let the Property or take in lodgers without the Lender's consent;

(5)   comply with all conditions and restrictions affecting the Property as set out in the title deeds;

(6)   [anything else]

5.   The standard security gives the Lender a [first] charge over the Property as security for all the sums mentioned in paragraph 3 above. You could lose the Property if the Borrower's business does not prosper, or if the borrowing is increased unwisely. This is because, if any loan repayment or interest charge is not paid on time, the Lender would be entitled to call up the standard security and take court proceedings to evict you and any other occupiers from the Property and sell the Property in order to obtain repayment.

6.   [The Lender reserves the right to transfer the benefit of the standard security to another lender.]

7.   [In addition, the mortgage will contain an obligation by you to pay all sums falling within paragraph 3 above if the Borrower fails to pay them [up to a maximum of £   plus interest charged by the Lender]. This means that [up to that level] you will be a guarantor for the liabilities of the Borrower to the Lender, you will be personally liable for those sums, you could be sued by the Lender for them and, if the value of the Property and your other assets is insufficient to meet those sums, you could be made bankrupt as well as losing the Property.]

8.   [Any other feature of the facility needing comment?]

The above legal advice relates to the effect of the mortgage documents and the types of risks that arise. [However, [I am] [we are] not qualified to assess the likelihood of those risks actually materialising. That depends largely on the financial standing and prospects of the Borrower [and his business], although you should also consider whether the sums secured could be repaid from the sale value of the Property and your other assets. You confirmed when we met that you were willing to sign [the mortgage documentation] without first assessing the risks by taking on those important financial aspects from a chartered accountant or other qualified professional financial adviser [independent of the Borrower].]

Please sign the document at the end of the enclosed copy of this letter to acknowledge that you have been given, and have understood, this advice, that you are willing to enter into the mortgage and that you will not require the Lender to vary any of the terms. [I] [We] will retain the signed documentation in this office and will only release it to the Lender's solicitors on receipt of the signed duplicate letter.

Yours

ACKNOWLEDGMENT

I confirm that I have read this letter and have received and understood the advice given in it. I confirm that I have decided, on my own free will, to enter into the mortgage, I do not require the Lender to vary any of the terms, [I do not required any further legal advice,] and I agreed that the Lender may be told that I have received the advice in this letter.

Signed:

                                                                Date:

This is a valuable style although there might be scope for making it yet clearer and more client-orientated. The mixed use of English and Scottish terminology might also be reviewed.

Sale at an undervalue

There is a gulf between our law of heritable security and mortgage law in England and English-influenced systems. Nevertheless sometimes there are cases worth noting. For instance *Bisset v Standard Property Investment plc*[1] was decided to a large extent on the basis of an Australian case, *Commercial and General Acceptance Ltd v Nixon*.[2] A new decision of the Privy Council on New Zealand law seems worth noting: *Newport Farm Ltd v Damesh Holdings Ltd*.[3]

A mortgage was enforced by sale. Under s 103A of New Zealand's Property Act 1952, corresponding to our s 27 of the Conveyancing and Feudal Reform (Scotland) Act 1970:

> a mortgagee who exercised a power of sale of land or other mortgaged property . . . owes a duty to the mortgagor to take reasonable care to obtain the best price reasonably obtainable as at the time of sale.

The mortgagors sued the mortgagees for alleged breach of this obligation. The case was complex, and we merely quote the joint opinion of the Judicial Committee:[4]

---

1 *Bisset v Standard Property Investment plc* 1999 GWD 26-1253.
2 *Commercial and General Acceptance Ltd v Nixon* [1983] 152 CLR 491. See *Conveyancing 1999* p 52.
3 *Newport Farm Ltd v Damesh Holdings Ltd* [2003] UKPC 54, [2003] All ER (D) 114.
4 [2003] UKPC 54 at para [22].

On the findings of the trial judge, Hansen J, the $13.7 million price was the market value of the property at the time of sale. So an inquiry as to damages would produce a nil result. Their Lordships think that the appellant's submissions proceed upon a mistaken premise as to the nature of the section 103A duty. Section 103A codifies the duty which, under the general law, a mortgagee exercising a power of sale would be taken to owe to the mortgagor (see *Cuckmere Brick Co Ltd v Mutual Finance Ltd* [1971] Ch 949). It does not produce a duty breach of which is actionable without proof of damage. If a mortgagor wants an inquiry as to damages for breach of the section 103A duty, the mortgagor must ... satisfy the court that it has suffered at least some damage. Here, on the findings of Hansen J, AFL and the appellants have failed to show either that a sale at a price of $13.7 million was a sale below market value or that any other type of sale would have produced any better price. The action fails on this ground, too ....

We consider that this is also Scots law. We draw attention to *Newport* because some pursuers think it sufficient to plead that the heritable creditor did not conduct the sale properly. In our view, if the sale achieved a fair market value, no damages will be due, even if the sale was not carried out properly. The starting point of the pursuer's case has to be loss caused by a sale at undervalue. Only if that can be established does it become relevant to determine whether that loss was attributable to the heritable creditor's fault.

Encroachment

The facts of *Young v West*[1] are an extreme example of a problem not in itself uncommon. The pursuer and the defender owned adjoining properties on Great Western Road, Buckie. The pursuer had owned the property since 1966, and his parents had owned it before him. Before that it was owned by sea scouts. The sea scouts ran a fence, to the north and west, 12 feet inside the legal boundaries of the property. The 12-feet strip beyond the fence but within the boundaries was then used for marching practice. The result, once the marching stopped and the property changed hands, was to mislead. From a visual inspection the western boundary – the boundary with which the present dispute was concerned – appeared to be the fence. But the legal boundary lay a further 12 feet to the west. The pursuer knew the truth but, for reasons which are unclear, seems to have kept it to himself.

Over time the neighbours to the west began to make use of the strip. At first this was for parking. Later they erected a fence of their own near the pursuer's fence. In 1995 the defender acquired the property. He obtained planning permission and began building. The works included a drive-through car-wash which was to be built partly on the strip. The pursuer was aware of the plans, and of the building work which followed. Yet it was not until much of the car-wash had been installed that he voiced his objections and pointed out that the strip was his.

---

1 *Young v West* (A128/98) (3 September 2003, unreported), Elgin Sheriff Court.

At that point the defender offered to buy the strip. The pursuer refused to sell. The strip was, it seems, of no particular value to him. To the defender, however, it was of great value. It was not clear that the car-wash could be satisfactorily located elsewhere on his land, but in any event to do so would cost between £13,000 and £20,000.

The pursuer sought declarator of ownership and removal of the encroachment. In the first crave he was successful. The current stage of litigation concerned the second crave. Two main arguments were open to the defender. One was that, by his silence, the pursuer had acquiesced in the encroachment and was now personally barred from objecting. The other was that the court should exercise its equitable power to refuse the extreme remedy of requiring the removal of the encroachment. The defender failed with the first but succeeded with the second.

The failure in respect of the first is surprising. Standing back and allowing an encroachment to take place, at considerable expense, before finally entering objections is the very essence of acquiescence. The sheriff, however, was influenced by the fact that the defender thought all along that the strip was his. Acquiescence, in the sheriff's view, was a question of implied consent; and for the defender to believe that the pursuer was consenting to the encroachment it was first necessary for him to know that the strip was not his, and hence that consent was necessary at all. This analysis seems open to question. It would be a strange doctrine which protected an encroacher when he was in bad faith – knowingly building on someone else's land – but not when he was in good faith. But in any event the sheriff was looking at the doctrine from the wrong end. The question was not, what did the defender think? but rather, what did the pursuer do? Personal bar here is about the owner's conduct and not about the encroacher's mental state. What the pursuer did was to give the impression that he had no interest in the strip. As a result the defender incurred significant expenditure. That seems a clear case of acquiescence.[1]

The second argument, however, succeeded. It is well-established that a court is not bound to order the removal of an encroachment, and it will not do so where this is unreasonable having regard to factors such as (1) whether removal would cause significant loss; (2) whether the encroacher was in good faith; (3) the value of the land to the owner compared to its value to the encroacher; (4) whether the removal of the encroachment would adversely affect the (legitimate) use being made by the encroacher of his own land; and (5) the wider interests of the community.[2] The defender succeeded on all of these grounds. Removal would be expensive. The encroachment was innocent. The strip was of little value to the pursuer. To remove the car-wash would be to interfere substantially with the defender's business. And finally, in the sheriff's words, 'it is arguable that if the order were granted the motoring community of Buckie and district would be denied the convenience and ease of having their cars washed without physical

---

1 Elspeth Reid 'Personal Bar: Case Law in Search of Principle' (2003) 7 *Edinburgh Law Review* 340, 353 n 72.

2 The leading modern case is *Anderson v Brattisani's* 1978 SLT (Notes) 42.

exertion'.[1] The sheriff refused the remedy and allowed the car-wash to stay in place.

Some loose ends remain. One is whether the pursuer will now be able to claim damages in respect of the encroachment – a normal consequence of a refusal of the remedy of removal.[2] Such a claim would have been barred by acquiescence, but there was held to be no acquiescence.

Another is the use of the car-wash. Removal was refused, and so was interdict against use. Yet the strip remained the property of the pursuer.[3] The car-wash could, it seems, stay in place and indeed by accession presumably belonged to the pursuer. It is not clear on what legal basis it could now be used by the defender and his customers, at least in the absence of a finding of personal bar.[4]

A third is the long-term future of the encroachment. If the strip, and the car-wash, remained the pursuer's, he could sell them to a third party. What then? As a general rule, personal bar cannot be pled against third parties. The same may be true of the equitable defence against removal. Although the law is uncertain, therefore, it seems that the future of the car-wash is not assured. Indeed, we understand that the pursuer has not only appealed, but that he has raised a separate action for interdict against the defender's putting in a water supply into the car-wash, and that interdict has been granted. The reality is that, even if an order for removal is refused, the legal position of an encroacher is usually weak. Only acquisition of the land provides a stable, long-term solution.

Building (Scotland) Act 2003

The Building (Scotland) Act 2003 (asp 8) is the first major reform in this area since the Building (Scotland) Act 1959, and the 1959 Act is prospectively repealed by the 2003 Act. The current plan is to bring the new Act into force in 2005. It may be worth recalling that the 1959 Act itself did not come into force until 1964.

The basic idea of (1) building regulations, (2) building warrants, (3) completion certificates and (4) enforcement powers continues. But much else changes. One of the drivers for the reform was the need to make the Scottish system compliant with EU law, under which there must be standardisation of rules about 'construction products'.

---

1 *Young v West* (A128/98) (3 September 2003, unreported) at para 6.3.
2 K G C Reid *The Law of Property in Scotland* (1996) para 178. And see para 6.4 of the sheriff's decision: 'The issue of possible equitable compensation was not canvassed before me and I have no information upon which to make any finding in that regard. That said, however, it occurs to me that the measure of equitable compensation to the Pursuer, if it were to arise, might be payment of the value of the strip (ignoring the Defender's works thereon) by the Defender in consideration of a conveyance thereof to the Defender.'
3 *Young v West* (A128/98) (3 September 2003, unreported) at para 6.1.
4 K G C Reid *The Law of Property in Scotland* (1996) para 176.

Scottish Building Standards Agency (SBSA)

Although the Building (Scotland) Act 2003 is silent about this agency, SBSA will be 'the central cog' in the new system.[1] The SBSA will be a non-statutory department of the Executive, so that when the Act refers to the Scottish Ministers, in practice their functions will be exercised by the SBSA.

Continuing requirements

Section 2 of the Building (Scotland) Act 2003 says that 'building regulations may impose on owners of buildings to which such regulations apply such continuing requirements as the Scottish Ministers consider appropriate for securing that the purposes of any designated provision of the regulations are not frustrated'. This is a new provision. The idea is not that 'continuing requirements' are imposed on individual buildings when building warrant is granted. Rather, it is that the building regulations themselves can impose continuing requirements. What, in practical terms, the scope of the new provision is likely to be is unclear.

Guidance documents

A major feature of the legislation is the replacement of compulsory technical standards by non-mandatory guidance documents. These will provide what the Building (Scotland) Act 2003 calls 'practical guidance with respect to the requirements of any provision of building regulations'.[2] The new system will thus be more flexible than the existing one. A question arises as to the status of guidance documents. Section 5 says that 'proof of compliance ... may be relied on in any proceedings ... as tending to negative any liability for an alleged contravention of building regulations'. This convoluted formula seems to mean, roughly speaking, that if work complies with the guidance documents then it presumptively complies with the regulations.[3]

Building standards assessments

Section 6 of the Building (Scotland) Act 2003 provides that an owner can ask the local authority to assess his building for compliance, thus putting on a statutory basis what already happens in practice. The section does not provide as such for a statement of no enforcement action (ie a comfort letter) but it seems that that is what is intended. An interesting feature of s 6 is that Ministers are empowered to

---

1 The expression is that of Brandon J Malone in his annotations in *Current Law Statutes*, to which we are much indebted.
2 Building (Scotland) Act 2003, s 4(1).
3 But what the formula means *precisely* is another question. To define the status of the guidance documents in terms of 'proceedings' seems topsy-turvy. Their status, whatever it is, must logically pre-date any proceedings.

make a statutory instrument limiting the period of time covered, so that, for instance, an assessment would not mention a failure to obtain a building warrant for works done more than x years ago.

Verifiers and certifiers

'Verifiers' and 'certifiers' are new species, and certifiers are themselves divided into 'approved certifiers of design' and 'approved certifiers of construction'. The new system represents a radical change, for whereas these roles have tradition-ally been performed by local authorities, in future other persons may be able to perform them.

A verifier is a person who issues building warrants and completion certificates. This is a public-law role and thus verifiers will be appointed by the Scottish Ministers – in practice by the Scottish Building Standards Agency.[1] They may be local authorities or individuals or companies. It is understood that, to begin with, Ministers will appoint only local authorities.

Certifiers will also be appointed by the Scottish Ministers. They are not a necessary part of the system, for they need not be used at all. But if an application for a warrant is accompanied by a certificate from an approved certifier of design, certifying that the plans conform to building regulations, then the verifier 'must accept the certificate as conclusive of the facts to which it relates'.[2] Likewise, at the completion certificate stage a verifier must accept as conclusive the certification of an approved certifier of construction.[3] This system of certifiers is controversial. There are concerns that pressure from clients will mean that their impartiality may be open to question.

Building Standards Register (BSR)

The Building (Scotland) Act 2003 aims to make information more readily avail-able to interested parties. Section 24 provides for a register of information about building warrants and completion certificates. The register will not be a single national register but rather a series of local ones, one for each local authority. The name will be the Building Standards Register. How the BSR will fit in to ordinary conveyancing practice remains to be seen. One possibility is that a search of the register will become a standard part of the purchaser's infor-mation pack,[4] if that system establishes itself, perhaps followed by an updated search after conclusion of missives. But this is to speculate. Much will depend on the cost of searches. At all events one suspects that the new system will be welcomed by conveyancers.

---

1 They can either be appointed directly or they can acquire their status under an 'approved scheme'. The same is true of certifiers.
2 Building (Scotland) Act 2003, s 11(3).
3 B(S)A 2003, s 19(3).
4 Discussed below in relation to the Housing Improvement Task Force.

Statutory notices

Section 87(1) of the Civic Government (Scotland) Act 1982 is repealed and replaced by s 28 of the Building (Scotland) Act 2003. The substance of the provisions remains the same.

Civil liability

A new feature of the Building (Scotland) Act 2003 is that 'breach of a duty imposed by building regulations, so far as it causes damage, is actionable, except in so far as the regulations otherwise provide'.[1] Much will depend on the extent to which the future regulations do otherwise provide.

Registration of title

Losing servitudes, claiming indemnity

The interaction of servitudes with registration of title is awkward and sometimes unclear. Partly this is because servitudes can be created off the Register – by prescription or by implied grant – and, once so created, tend to stay off the Register. Indeed the Keeper is no longer willing to include on the Register servitudes said to have been created by prescription unless there is a declarator to that effect.[2] In relation to the servient tenement, therefore, servitudes are classified as overriding interests – real rights which may affect the land without appearing on the Register.

But of course servitudes often do appear on the Register. If a servitude appears in a Sasine title then, on first registration, it is likely to reappear on the Land Register. Or if a servitude is created of new in the disposition inducing first registration or in some later deed, then it too will normally appear on the Register. For a land certificate to include a servitude is, therefore, nothing out of the ordinary. But to what extent can such inclusion be relied upon? Is the mention of a servitude conclusive evidence that it exists? What if the underlying deeds do not support the right? Could the resulting inaccuracy on the Register then be rectified? And if so, does this mean that a person acquiring land which bears to be the dominant tenement cannot take the Register at face value but must rummage around in the prior deeds?

These reflections are prompted by an important decision of the Lands Tribunal, *Griffiths v The Keeper of the Registers of Scotland.*[3] The facts were unremarkable. On

---

1 Building (Scotland) Act 2003, s 51. The word 'actionable' prefers remedies to rights and is to be regretted in a Scottish statute.
2 Registers of Scotland *Registration of Title Practice Book* (2nd edn, 2000) paras 6.54–6.58.
3 *Griffiths v The Keeper of the Registers of Scotland* (20 December 2002, unreported), Lands Tribunal. See also p 62 above.

the face of the Register, the titles of both halves of a semi-detached house were disarmingly consistent. On the title sheet of one was noted, in the property section, a servitude of way in respect of land forming part of the other; and there was a matching entry in the burdens section of the title sheet of the other.[1] Anyone buying the dominant property would have been reassured and would probably have made no further inquiries. It turned out, however, that the supposed servitude, although part of the Sasine titles for many years, had not been validly created. Accordingly, the owner of the apparently burdened property sought to have the servitude removed from the Register.

Several different arguments were canvassed. In the end, however, the legal analysis was relatively straightforward. The Register was inaccurate in showing a servitude which had not been properly constituted. In principle an inaccuracy can be corrected by rectification.[2] But the Register cannot be rectified to the prejudice of a proprietor in possession, except in certain limited circumstances, none of which applied here.[3] Rectification would prejudice the holder of the servitude. The legal question was whether such a person could be said to be a 'proprietor in possession'.

The Land Registration (Scotland) Act 1979 does not define 'proprietor in possession'. But in the light of *Kaur v Singh*[4] it seems that whether a person is a 'proprietor' depends on the right in land in respect of which the proprietorship is said to exist. The essential distinction is between those rights – ownership and long lease – which command their own title sheet, and those other rights which do not. Thus the owner of land, or a lessee under a long lease, is a 'proprietor' within the meaning of the 1979 Act and hence, if in possession, is a 'proprietor in possession'. But a heritable creditor – the particular example litigated in *Kaur v Singh* – is not a 'proprietor' and hence is not protected against rectification.

It has not been clear how a servitude might fit into this analysis. On the one hand, a servitude does not command its own title sheet. But, almost uniquely among real rights, a servitude is not freestanding in nature but can only be held by a person who is at the same time the owner of land (ie of the dominant tenement). And since such a person is necessarily a 'proprietor' *of that land*, the way is open to argue that he or she is a 'proprietor' also for the purposes of the servitude. A version of this argument found favour in *Mutch v Mavisbank Properties Ltd*.[5] According to the sheriff principal in that case:[6]

I am rather inclined to the view that in a case where the Keeper is being asked to rectify the Register by deleting a servitude right of access from the title sheet, a dominant proprietor would in normal circumstances be 'prejudiced' and would as a matter of parliamentary intention fall to be regarded as a 'proprietor in possession'.

---

1 Both titles were in fact long leases.
2 Land Registration (Scotland) Act 1979, s 9(1).
3 LR(S)A 1979, s 9(3).
4 *Kaur v Singh* 1999 SC 180.
5 *Mutch v Mavisbank Properties Ltd* 2002 SLT (Sh Ct) 91. See *Conveyancing 2002* pp 85–6.
6 Sheriff Principal E F Bowen QC at p 94I.

These remarks, however, were *obiter*. In *Griffiths* the matter fell to be decided for the first time.

The Lands Tribunal considered that the holder of a servitude was not a 'proprietor', and so could not be a proprietor in possession. That result followed, it was said, both from the decision in *Kaur v Singh* and from the statutory language. It also followed as a matter of legal policy:[1]

> Loss of an apparent servitude could have a significant adverse effect on an occupier's enjoyment of his land ... This, however, is not the equivalent of being ejected from the land.

Accordingly, in a case such as the present, where the servitude was not supported by the underlying deeds, the Register could be rectified. Thus servitudes are always vulnerable to rectification.

Typically, of course, the pain of rectification is soothed by the balm of indemnity. The person loses the right but receives its monetary value. To this comforting principle, however, servitudes may constitute an unwelcome exception. Section 12(3) of the Land Registration (Scotland) Act 1979 contains a long list of circumstances in which, even in the absence of an exclusion of indemnity, no indemnity will be paid. In *Griffiths* the Tribunal's attention was drawn to para (g), which avoids indemnity where

> the loss arises from inability to enforce a real burden or condition entered in the Register, unless the Keeper expressly assumes responsibility for the enforceability of that burden or condition.

Needless to say, it is almost unknown for the Keeper expressly to assume such responsibility. None was assumed in the present case.

It is possible that s 12(3)(g) of the 1979 Act prevents a claim for indemnity in a case such as the present. That was the suggestion made in *Griffiths* although the point was not a matter for decision and was perhaps not fully argued. If correct, however, this would be an unfortunate result. To lose a servitude is bad enough. To lose it without the prospect of indemnity could lead to substantial loss. It would be to take servitudes more or less outside the system of registration of title. It would leave an acquirer for whom the existence of a particular servitude was important with little choice but to go behind the Register and examine the relevant Sasine deeds – a result which it was the purpose of registration of title to avoid.

Our view, however, is that s 12(3)(g) of the 1979 Act does not operate on the facts of *Griffiths*, for three reasons. In the first place, it is unclear that a servitude qualifies as a 'real burden or condition' – the expression used in s 12(3)(g) – at all, although in *Griffiths* it was conceded that it did so qualify. It may be noted, for

---

1 *Griffiths v The Keeper of the Registers of Scotland* (20 December 2002, unreported), p 27 of the transcript.

example, that the word 'servitude' appears elsewhere in s 12(3), in a provision shortly to be mentioned.

Secondly, it is unclear that the loss in question would arise from 'inability to enforce' a servitude 'entered on the Register'. This is because, for as long as the servitude remained on the Register, it would be enforceable, notwithstanding the shortcomings of the underlying deeds. This is because title flows from the Register, and according to the Register the servitude exists. Thus it is only on removal of the servitude from the Register, following rectification, that it would cease to be enforceable. The real cause of the loss, on this view, is not the presence on the Register of an unenforceable right but rather the subsequent absence from the Register of a right which was previously enforceable.[1]

Thirdly, notice must be taken of a different paragraph of s 12(3): para (l). This excludes entitlement to indemnity where

> the claimant is the proprietor of the dominant tenement in a servitude, except insofar as the claim may relate to the validity of the constitution of that servitude.

In *Griffiths* the claim of the servitude holder, following rectification, would indeed 'relate to the validity of the constitution of that servitude'. It is necessary to pay close attention to the wording of s 12(3)(l) of the 1979 Act. It is does not state, as a positive rule, that claims of this kind *will* give rise to indemnity. Rather it states merely that such claims do not fall under the particular exclusion of indemnity provided for by s 12(3)(l); and strictly, there is nothing to prevent such claims being excluded by a different paragraph of s 12(3) – such as para (g). Yet, as a matter of statutory construction, it is difficult to believe that claims in relation to the constitution of servitudes would have been so carefully detached from para (l) if the intention had simply been that they should be denied under a different paragraph. A more plausible view is that such claims were intended to attract payment of indemnity all along.

Possessing river beds

In *Safeway Stores plc v Tesco Stores Ltd*[2] Safeway acquired property at Lonend, Paisley, its title being registered on 8 October 1997 under title number REN 56654. This was not a first registration: the registered title dated from 1984. At that time the southern boundary of the property, at a particular point, was the mid-line of

---

1 It should not be thought that this interpretation removes all content from s 12(3)(g) of the Land Registration (Scotland) Act 1979. The provision would remain important where a real burden or servitude was shown on the Register but was nonetheless unenforceable. That might be because the burden or servitude had never been enforceable, typically because it was of a type which was incapable of being constituted as a real burden or servitude. The proviso to s 3(1) of the 1979 Act prevents the creation of an enforceable right in such circumstances. Alternatively, the right might have been enforceable initially but thereafter ceased to be so, for example because it had prescribed.

2 *Safeway Stores plc v Tesco Stores Ltd* 2003 GWD 20-610.

a river, the White Cart Water. Shortly before Safeway's acquisition, however, this boundary in the title sheet was altered so that it extended two metres beyond the mid-line. The alteration was done by the Keeper as part of the digital conversion of the map base and without reference to any of the owners. It was both mistaken and, for some time, unnoticed. In acquiring the property, Safeway was quite unaware of the new boundary to the south.

The new area thus added to title number REN 56654 was, at that time, held on a Sasine title, and later in the same year the whole land held under that title was conveyed to Tesco, thus inducing first registration. At this point the problem began to emerge. Tesco noticed the potential title overlap and began negotiations with the Keeper to ensure that the disputed area was included in its own title sheet. At the same time Safeway had discovered, to its surprise, that its southern boundary extended further than it had thought. This was of considerable commercial importance. Safeway was to build a supermarket. A condition of planning permission was that it would construct a new bridge. As the title had originally stood, only an expensive curved bridge would have been possible. The revised boundaries allowed a cheaper straight bridge.

At one level at least, the resulting legal dispute was relatively straightforward. When Safeway's title was registered on 8 October 1997 the disputed strip was included in the title plan. Hence, as a matter of law, Safeway became owners of that strip.[1] But since the inclusion of the strip was the result of administrative error, the Register was inaccurate and could, in principle, be rectified.[2] Tesco therefore applied for rectification.[3] At this point it came up against the familiar problem of the proprietor in possession. Rectification cannot normally be carried out if it would prejudice a proprietor in possession.[4] But was Safeway in possession? On this issue the case largely turned.

It is difficult to possess a river bed but Tesco did their best. On 7 August 1998 Tesco had marker posts placed on the bed, including two in the disputed area. This was done using a crane supervised by an engineer in a boat. The poles

---

1 Land Registration (Scotland) Act 1979, s 3(1)(a).
2 Actually it is possible to argue that it was not inaccurate in the hands of Safeway. When the alteration was first made, the Register was certainly inaccurate. But Safeway did not own at that time. Safeway acquired the property subsequently, from a person who, on the face of the Register, owned the disputed area. If it is accepted that the initial alteration of the Register had the effect of conferring ownership (an issue discussed below), it would follow that Safeway took the title from the then-owner, under a disposition which included the disputed area. See Scottish Law Commission *Discussion Paper on Land Registration: Void and Voidable Titles* (Scot Law Com DP No 125, 2004; available on www.scotlawcom.gov.uk) paras 5.17–5.19.
3 Since, however, Tesco's title derived from an *a non domino* conveyance, it is not clear why allocating the disputed strip to Tesco was any less of an 'inaccuracy' than leaving it with Safeway. See *Conveyancing 2001* pp 110–12. But this point seems not to have been argued.
4 LR(S)A 1979, s 9(3)(a). There are exceptions but none was applicable. In particular the inaccuracy could not be said to have caused by Safeway's fraud or carelessness: s 9(3)(a)(iii). There was no question of fraud. It was not 'careless' of Safeway to fail to inform themselves as to the southern boundary; and even if they had so informed themselves it would not have been 'careless' to rely on the title plan on the Register: see *Dougbar Properties Ltd v Keeper of the Registers of Scotland* 1999 SC 513. Finally, and in any event, the inaccuracy was not 'caused' by Safeway but by the Keeper.

carried notices reading 'Private property of Tesco Stores Ltd. Unauthorised access prohibited'. At this stage Tesco was unaware of the mistake in the title. When the two crucial poles were washed away during the winter they were replaced, on 21 May 1999, with more robust posts which were placed on sandbags by divers. A month later Safeway removed these posts and re-positioned them on the part of the river which indisputably belonged to Tesco.[1] This 'tennis match' (in the phrase of counsel for Safeway) might have gone on indefinitely. Instead the parties litigated.

If the facts did not disclose unequivocal possession by either party, that was more serious for Safeway than for Tesco. In order for Tesco's application for rectification to succeed it was not necessary to show that it possessed but merely that Safeway did not. It was argued strongly for Safeway that possession of part of a property must be treated as possession of the whole, at least where the boundaries were clear. By possessing other parts of the subjects registered under title number REN 56654 Safeway must be taken to have possessed up to the boundary as shown on the title plan. This argument failed before the Lands Tribunal[2] and has failed again before an Extra Division of the Court of Session. Special considerations applied, it was said, in the evaluation of possession for the purposes of the Land Registration (Scotland) Act 1979:[3]

[I]t is necessary, in the circumstances of this case, to make some attempt to divine what the legislature had in mind by a proprietor 'in possession' who *ex hypothesi* does not 'truly' have the right accorded to him on the Register but whose possession (and registered proprietorship) is nonetheless, as a matter of policy, not to be disturbed. In my view the term 'in possession' in this statutory context imports some significant element of physical control, combined with the relevant intent; it suggests actual use or enjoyment, to a more than minimal extent, of the subjects in question as one's own. It is a 'proprietor' who has, on the faith of the Register, had such enjoyment or use who is protected against rectification. A 'proprietor' who has not had such enjoyment or use is not so protected and may require to seek his remedy, if any, in the form of indemnity.

It could not therefore be assumed that the normal rules of possession always applied, or those developed in the context of positive prescription. Given the nature of the disputed area, it had been reasonable for the Lands Tribunal not to apply the rule that possession of part was possession of the whole, and once this rule was rejected it became necessary to show specific possessory acts. There was none other than the removal, late in the day, of Tesco's poles. This did not amount to possession of the disputed area. Nor did the mere drawing up of plans to use this area for the projected bridge. Since, therefore, Safeway was not proprietor in possession, rectification could proceed.

---

1 These oscillating possessory acts bring to mind the various changes of locks in *Kaur v Singh* 1999 SC 180.
2 *Tesco Stores Ltd v Keeper of the Registers of Scotland* 2001 SLT (Lands Tr) 23. See *Conveyancing 2001* pp 108–15.
3 *Safeway Stores plc v Tesco Stores Ltd* 2003 GWD 20-610 at para [77] per Lord Hamilton.

While, however, Tesco was successful, one of its arguments was not. Tesco emphasised that the addition to the Safeway title had occurred by accident and not by registration. In respect of that addition, therefore, they were not truly 'proprietors'. Only registration could confer that status. And if Safeway was not 'proprietor', nor was it 'proprietor in possession'. Hence rectification could proceed without an inquiry into possession. This argument has a certain plausibility.[1] Ownership is conferred by s 3(1) of the Land Registration (Scotland) Act 1979, but that section requires an act of registration. If land is added to a title merely by accident, unconnected with an application for registration, there is no statutory basis for supposing that ownership is thereby conferred. But that analysis, if correct, would only cover the period between the original mapping error and the registration of Safeway's title. For Safeway was registered as owner of the whole subjects, including the area added by accident; and on registration ownership was, necessarily, acquired. The rejection of Tesco's argument by the court was not, however, on this ground. The court's view was that the manner of acquisition was altogether irrelevant for the purposes of s 9: '[i]f an inaccuracy emerges, the manner in which it first arose is of no importance'.[2]

In the litigation, one factor was largely overlooked. This was that title to the disputed area was registered not once but twice. First it was registered on 8 October 1997 in Safeway's name under title number REN 56654; and then it was registered again in September 1998 in Tesco's name under title number REN 93746. The idea that the same property can be registered under two different title sheets (other than by inadvertence) is difficult to grasp. Normally, of course, it would not occur. Initially indeed the disputed area was not included under REN 93746 but it was added a few months later following representations by Tesco. A practical justification is that it allowed prescription to run.[3] But whatever the justification, the result was to move into uncharted waters.[4] If the same land is registered under two separate titles, where does ownership lie? On the face of the Register the land belonged to Safeway, and at the same time and quite separately it belonged also to Tesco. It is true that the Tesco title contained the following, rather curious, notice:

> As regards the part tinted blue on the Title Plan [ie the disputed area], Indemnity is excluded in terms of Section 12(2) of the Land Registration (Scotland) Act 1979 in respect that the said part tinted blue was registered under Title Number REN 56654 on 8 October 1997 and ranks prior to the Disposition to Tesco Stores Limited registered 14 May 1998 on which the entitlement of the said Tesco Stores Limited was founded.

---

1 *Conveyancing 2001* pp 114–5.
2 *Safeway Stores plc v Tesco Stores Ltd* 2003 GWD 20-610 at para [71] per Lord Hamilton.
3 Indeed the Keeper's practice in this area, understandably enough, seems intended to reproduce the effect of the Sasine system. The grantee is given the opportunity of prescription, but until prescription has run he is not regarded as, properly speaking, the owner. The difficulty is that on registration a person *is* the owner, whatever the note excluding indemnity might say.
4 Note however that much the same issue arises if, following a conveyance *a non domino*, the Keeper enters the name of the disponee without at the same time removing the name of the previous owner. For a discussion, see G L Gretton and K G C Reid *Conveyancing* (2nd edn, 1999) para 8.15.

But indemnity is not the same thing as title. The fact that title is not guaranteed has no bearing on its validity. Section 12 of the Land Registration (Scotland) Act 1979 operates separately from s 3.

The notice did at least indicate the Keeper's view of matters. The owner was Safeway, not Tesco. The first to register was preferred to the second. That view seems to have been accepted in the litigation: hence the need for rectification. Probably it is incorrect. Admittedly the issue is one of considerable difficulty and only limited guidance can be found from the 1979 Act.[1] But the balance of argument strongly favours the view that the last to register – Tesco in this case – is the owner.[2]

To understand why it is necessary to examine once again the history of the title. Until 1997 the disputed area was the property of an unknown third party. The position changed when, on 8 October 1997, Safeway was registered as owner. Here the effect of s 3(1)(a) of the 1979 Act is clear. Registration vests in the applicant 'a real right in and to the interest'; and this real right (in this case, of ownership) arises irrespective of the prior state of the title. Following registration, the Register might be inaccurate. There might be exclusion of indemnity. But the act of registration confers ownership on the person registered as proprietor. Safeway thus became owner on 8 October 1997. So matters remained until September 1998 and the registration in favour of Tesco.

Registration in favour of Tesco also triggered s 3(1)(a). On registration Tesco, equally, became owner of the disputed area. Because only one title of ownership is possible at any one time,[3] the fact that Tesco became owner meant that Safeway had ceased to be owner.[4] Section 3(1)(a), it will be noted, produces a single rather than a continuing effect. It made Safeway owner but it did not protect that ownership in the future. If someone else became owner – eg by voluntary transfer by Safeway – then Safeway's own title would be lost.

The Land Registration (Scotland) Act 1979 admits of one possible counter-argument. In terms of s 7(2) 'titles to registered interests in land shall rank according to the date of registration of those interests'. The word 'rank' here recalls the Keeper's note in excluding indemnity. The argument is simple. Rights rank in the order of registration; and since Safeway registered first, its title is to be preferred to that of Tesco. Almost certainly the argument is mistaken, for two reasons.

First, s 3(1)(a) of the 1979 Act is not qualified by s 7. This is not merely the technical argument that s 3 is not declared to be subject to s 7 (although that

---

1 One reason for this is that the idea of two concurrent registrations in respect of the same property can hardly have been in the minds of those devising the scheme.
2 K G C Reid *The Law of Property in Scotland* (1996) para 685.
3 *Sharp v Thomson* 1995 SC 455 at 469F per Lord President Hope. See *Safeway Stores plc v Tesco Stores Ltd* 2003 GWD 20-610 at para [13].
4 If A becomes owner of property owned by B, B must cease to be owner. So for example if A acquires ownership by positive prescription, B is no longer owner. In effect B has lost his ownership by positive (and not by negative) prescription.

is true). It is that it would make no sense if it were. Section 3(1)(a) conferred on Tesco a real right of ownership. That is not a right which could 'rank' behind some other real right of ownership. Ownership is all or nothing. To say that one right of ownership 'ranks' behind another is to say the impossible. A second-ranking right of ownership – if the idea could be imagined – would be no right at all but a simple nullity. That result cannot be reconciled with s 3(1)(a).

Secondly, and more broadly, s 7 is about ranking and hence only about those real rights – notably rights in security – which are capable of co-existing within a hierarchy. It has no application to exclusive rights such as ownership.[1]

If, however, Tesco were already owners, it would not matter that Safeway's title plan continued to show the disputed area. Any attempt by Safeway to use the disputed area could be met by interdict. Insofar as rectification was necessary, it was necessary only in respect in Tesco's own title, to the effect of striking out the Keeper's notice about indemnity.[2]

Housing Improvement Task Force

The Housing Improvement Task Force was set up by the Scottish Executive in December 2000.[3] Its remit focused on three main areas:

(1) houses and flats in need of repair in the owner-occupied sector;

(2) buying and selling of houses; and

(3) renting property in the private sector.

The first stage was to consider the legal, administrative and financial aspects of the current system. This stage was concerned with fact-finding rather than with recommendations, and was completed with the publication, in March 2002, of the Task Force's first report, *Issues in Improving Quality in Private Housing*.[4] In 2003 the second report was published. This makes recommendations for change. It is an 'upstream' report in the sense that it makes general policy recommendations but often says little about the details of implementation.[5] In other words, much additional work would be needed to translate the recommendations into legislation. And of course the recommendations will not necessarily be adopted by the

---

1 K G C Reid 'A Non Domino Conveyances and the Land Register' 1991 *Juridical Review* 79.
2 In fact rectification was also granted to that effect, although not for the reasons just advanced.
3 The Housing Improvement Task Force website is at www.scotland.gov.uk/hitf.
4 Noted in *Conveyancing 2002* pp 45–6.
5 The report is full of expressions such as 'key stakeholders', 'framework for delivery', 'integrated scheme', 'person-centred', 'appropriate mechanisms', 'client interest groups', 'partner organisations', 'forums' and so on. Some of the discussion in the report is in such general terms that it is hard to know what it really means in practical terms.

Ministers. Nevertheless, it would be surprising if at least some of the report were not to be implemented.

Some leading points of the second report[1] are as follows.[2]

Housing standards

The Housing (Scotland) Acts should be amended so as to make housing standards more demanding.

Single surveys

The solution to the problem of multiple surveys is a single survey commissioned by the seller.[3] The seller would pay, but would issue copies to prospective purchasers, on condition that they agree to reimburse the seller if they are the actual purchasers.[4] The survey type would be the Scheme 2 Homebuyer's Report and Valuation. To make the system work the surveyor would have to be an approved one. The surveyor might be required to add a guarantee against latent defects. The terms of the seller/surveyor contract would require careful consideration to define to what extent the surveyor would be liable, and to whom, but the report gives no details. The new system would be introduced on a voluntary basis, but if voluntary acceptance were not to happen then compulsion would be required. The expression used is 'sanctions for non-compliance'.[5] There is no discussion of what such sanctions might be. The first step would be a pilot scheme (see below).

---

1 Housing Improvement Task Force *Stewardship and Responsibility: A Policy Framework for Private Housing in Scotland* (ISBN 0 755 90723 X). The physical quality of the report is low, if Edinburgh University Library's copy is typical. Professor Gretton was the first person to open it. Every page fell out on being turned for the first time. A national task force is needed to tackle the appalling problems caused by badly-bound books, problems evidently caused by market failure and chronic under-investment in the physical quality of the nation's book stock. The process will begin by establishing a forum of key stakeholders in which a person-centred framework initiative can be developed with a view to targeted delivery. Local authority powers to prohibit the use of such books by private book-owners until they have been upgraded by a certified bookbinder will be central. 90% grants will be available on a means-tested basis.

2 The report has already received discussion in the legal press. See Brymer (2003) 63 *Greens Property Law Bulletin* 4; Lewin (2003) 48 *Journal of the Law Society of Scotland* Nov/60 and Dec/62; Swinton (2003) 71 *Scottish Law Gazette* 177.

3 This has already attracted hostile comment. In a letter published in the *Journal of the Law Society of Scotland* for December 2003 (p 10), Stuart M Bain observed: '[T]his perverse concept raises a plethora of completely unworkable issues. Do we really think a seller will stump up a further £300 (for the benefit of the purchaser) with, at most, a hazy expectation that it might be repaid? Are purchasers' solicitors really going to advise their client to tap into such a survey with all the nefarious implications for solicitor and client that would follow? Do we really, truly foresee the insurance industry picking up the tab under a "hidden defects guarantee" for a paltry £25 a pop in the current climate? Yeah . . . right.'

4 The report sees this as an important issue, but one imagines that the offer would simply say that the price would be deemed to include the cost of the survey.

5 Housing Improvement Task Force *Stewardship and Responsibility: A Policy Framework for Private Housing in Scotland* (2003) para 166.

Purchaser's information pack

Sellers would make available to prospective purchasers a 'purchaser's information pack', containing:[1]

(1) 'copies of any planning, list building consent and building warrants ...' Completion certificates are not mentioned;

(2) 'any guarantees for work carried out ...' including NHBC certificate if applicable;

(3) 'a copy of the land certificate or, where a certificate is not available, at least a summary of common repair and maintenance burdens attached to flatted properties';

(4) 'a summary note of any relevant property management arrangements which would include details of any property manager (name, contact address, fees) and if applicable, any owner's association ...';

(5) 'a Coal Authority Report if applicable'.

The idea of a property 'log book' recording work done on the property is one that is to be encouraged but this is not made a formal part of the recommendations.

The hope would be that the new system could be introduced on a voluntary basis, but if voluntary acceptance were not to happen then compulsion would be required. The first step would be a pilot scheme.

Closing dates

The possibility of forbidding the setting of early closing dates is considered but rejected. 'We concluded that changes along these lines would be heavy-handed, bureaucratic and out of proportion to the problem.'[2]

Blind bidding

The possibility of forbidding the blind bidding system is considered but rejected. One reason is that the existing system is well-established and understood. The second is that the existing system is not compulsory anyway. Why these points apply to blind bidding but not to other matters (eg the survey system) is not explained.

Upset levels

The alleged problem of low upset prices is considered.[3] The possibility of legislation to prohibit low upset prices is considered but rejected.

---

1 *Stewardship and Responsibility* Recommendation 34.
2 *Stewardship and Responsibility* para 189.
3 On which see further Stewart Brymer 'Low Upset Prices' (2003) 64 *Greens Property Law Bulletin* 7.

Standard-form missives

The possibility of standard-form missives is considered. Parties should be free to agree their own terms. However, it is noted that the Law Society of Scotland's Conveyancing Committee is looking at the possibility of developing standard terms and this initiative is welcomed.

Builders' missives

A number of possible problem areas in builders' missives are identified. Missives sometimes:

(1) provide for Deeds of Conditions, whose terms are often unavailable to buyers when missives are concluded;

(2) require deposits without satisfactory provision for what is to happen if the transaction does not proceed;

(3) require that the buyer must pay the price without the builder having to grant a valid disposition in exchange;

(4) provide for payment to the builder rather than to the builder's solicitor;

(5) say that the builder is not required to exhibit any necessary permissions under public law;

(6) provide that the builder is free to change the overall development;

(7) fail to give details about factoring arrangements;

(8) provide that the date of entry can be changed unilaterally by the builder;

(9) fail to give the buyer adequate protection outwith the NHBC scheme;

(10) prohibit retentions from the price, contrary to the norm in construction contracts, in which it is standard practice for a retention to be made for a defined period to cover potential defects.

The Task Force felt unable to give these issues detailed consideration. But it recommended that the Scottish Executive should review the issues with the object of 'brokering an agreement between the various parties'.[1] Should such a brokered agreement fail, then legislation would be advisable 'to put in place minimum safeguards for buyers'.[2]

Clarifying costs

Buyers and sellers do not always seem to know what the transaction is going to cost. No specific recommendation is made. However, the Law Society of

---

1 Housing Improvement Task Force *Stewardship and Responsibility: A Policy Framework for Private Housing in Scotland* (2003) para 207.
2 *Stewardship and Responsibility* para 208.

Scotland's proposal (now implemented)[1] to promulgate rules for sending out letters of engagement is welcomed.

The role of lenders

The possibility of involving secured lenders for the purpose of pressuring house owners to maintain their properties is considered but rejected.

Caveat emptor

The possibility of changing the law so that a seller would be deemed to warrant the physical quality of the property is considered but rejected. However, the rejection is only for second-hand houses. For new-build houses the report regards the point as an open one and it is to be part of the review urged on the Scottish Executive.

Complaints procedures

The report considers whether the avenues open to consumers who wish to complain are adequate. It concludes that in general they are. However, the report suggests that some changes may be required for non-solicitor estate agents.

Tax and benefits

This section of the report is headed 'tax and benefits' but some of the proposals perhaps do not fit in under those heads. The report recommends that the Scottish Executive should consider:[2]

(1)   changes to the VAT rules for repairs and maintenance;

(2)   changes to the tax rules for sinking funds;

(3)   changes to the Consumer Credit Act 1974 'in respect of small loans to reduce the administrative barriers' (the report gives no details; as it happens an overall review of the 1974 Act is being conducted at UK level);

(4)   'changing rules in respect of lending to facilitate the availability of loan products accessible by the Muslim community';[3]

(5)   'legislation for a new investment vehicle for indirect investment in existing good standard property';

---

1   Solicitors (Scotland) (Client Communication) (Residential Conveyancing) Practice Rules 2003, discussed on p 40.
2   *Stewardship and Responsibility* Recommendation 52.
3   This refers to the objection under Islamic law to usury, including payment of interest. The solution involves actual transfers of ownership back and forth. Without special provision, now made by the Finance Act 2003, ss 72 and 73, this would involve additional stamp duty land tax.

(6)   'introduction of rollover Capital Gains Tax relief on sales when reinvesting proceeds in other good quality properties';

(7)   'reduction in stamp duty on bulk transactions'.

Evidently most or all of these proposals would have to be implemented at Westminster, as the report itself observes.

Common repairs

This section is mainly concerned with tenemental property. The Report gives its support to the Tenements (Scotland) Bill, now in Parliament, and makes no other recommendations for legislative change.

Public assistance for repair and improvement of houses

This extensive section is about improvement grants. It would not involve new legislation.

Local authority powers

Various recommendations are made, generally in the direction of local authority powers.

Private landlords

'Private landlords need to increase their investment in repairs and maintenance.'[1] Legislation is recommended to enable landlords to be pressurised to do this, including the creation of a new Private Rented Housing Tribunal for Scotland.

The report considers whether there should be schemes of registration, of certification or of licensing for privately-rented properties. Licensing would be either by property or by landlord and would mean that it would be illegal to let a residential property without a licence. The report rejects all such schemes on a national basis but recommends that individual local authorities should be empowered to introduce such a scheme (whether registration, certification or full-scale licensing) within their own area.

Overall comments

The report contains matters of value and interest, but it tends also to be centrist and dirigiste. There is oddly little consideration of the economic impact of the proposed measures. The physical condition of a house is reflected in its capital and rental values. The worse the condition the lower the value; the better the

---

1 Housing Improvement Task Force *Stewardship and Responsibility: A Policy Framework for Private Housing in Scotland* (2003) para 437.

condition the higher the value. To improve the average quality of the housing stock is to increase capital values and thus also rental values, since rental values necessarily track capital values. The slogan 'improving housing quality' sounds good but it translates as 'increasing housing costs' which does not sound so good. That the market is already working well, and that the total national investment in the housing stock correctly reflects national choices as to the best uses of scarce resources, may or may not be true. A weakness of the report is that the issue is not considered.

The recommendation that sellers offer surveys and information packs is one that may catch on without the need for legislation. But if there is to be legislative compulsion it is not easy to see what form the legislation would take. Would these things be compulsory in all sales? What if the buyer is not interested in the seller's survey? What if there is a sale between members of the same family? What of a sale to a leaseholder who knows more about the property than the owner? What sanctions would there be? Fines? Jail? Would there be police swoops? Would enforcement officers pose as prospective buyers?

Inevitably too there are difficulties of detail. 'Copies of any planning, list building consent and building warrants . . .': but how far back? What about completion certificates? 'Any guarantees for work carried out . . .': again how far back? What if the guarantee has been lost? Does that mean that the property can never be sold? Such an owner would then regret that he had not obtained *unguaranteed* work. And what is meant by 'guarantee'? The common law always implies a warranty: is this included? What happens, more generally, if information is inaccurate, or accurate but incomplete? Apart from 'sanctions' will the buyer have redress?

Pilot scheme

The Task Force has established a Single Survey Steering Group.[1] The membership includes two representatives of the Law Society of Scotland.[2] A number of areas have been selected[3] and the pilot is planned to start during 2004. It is understood that it will be limited to the single survey idea, and will not extend – at least to begin with – to the idea of information packs. Participation will be voluntary, and that fact may limit the effectiveness.

Judicial rectification

Uninformed agreements: allowing a second chance?

Section 8 of the Law Reform (Miscellaneous Provisions) (Scotland) Act 1985 empowers a court to rectify a deed or other document intended to express or give

---

1 The Single Survey Steering Group has a website at www.scotland.gov.uk/sssg.
2 Stewart Brymer and Linsey Lewin.
3 The website has maps.

effect to an agreement if it can be shown that it fails to express accurately the common intention of the parties to the agreement. On this important provision the recent trend of decisions had been benign and accommodating. No error, it has seemed, is too foolish or fundamental that it cannot be put right by a stroke of the judicial pen. The latest decision from the Court of Session, however, suggests that there are limits to the role of s 8 of the 1985 Act. And it seems of significance that, in adopting a more circumscribed view of the provision, Lord Eassie stressed the commercial value of certainty, and the dangers of re-writing the agreed terms of contracts in order to take account of what may (or may not) have been the commercial objectives of the parties.[1]

The case, *Co-operative Wholesale Society Ltd v Ravenseft Properties Ltd*,[2] has already been reported at earlier stages.[3] The present, and it may well be final, stage of litigation involved a limited proof as to prior negotiations. The facts were these. The Co-op were tenants of Ravenseft (who were themselves tenants of a local authority). The subjects were a supermarket in a shopping centre in Dundee. The Co-op wished to sublet in turn to Shoprite, but Shoprite objected to certain terms of the Co-op lease. In particular they objected to clause (sixth), a keep-open clause. This provided that the tenants should commence trading:

> and shall continue to so use and occupy the premises and trade therefrom throughout the whole period of this sub-lease. If the tenants without first having obtained the written consent of the landlords, leave the premises unoccupied for a period exceeding twenty-one days, they shall be bound to indemnify the landlords for all loss or damage suffered by the landlords as a consequence of the failure by the tenants to occupy the premises, including without prejudice to the foregoing generality any loss or damage through depreciation in the capital value of the premises and/or whole subjects.

The Co-op, acting in effect as an intermediary between Shoprite and Ravenseft, persuaded Ravenseft that clause (sixth) should be deleted, and a Minute of Variation was duly drawn up and executed to that effect. Subsequently Ravenseft sold their interest in the shopping centre to Douglas Shelf Seven Ltd.[4] When, after a while, the shop ceased trading, the new landlords, founding on a second keep-open clause contained elsewhere in the Co-op lease, claimed damages of £700,000. In response, the Co-op sought rectification of the Minute of Variation. The parties' common intention, they argued, had been to delete the keep open clause. But, as the proof demonstrated, everyone had overlooked the second clause on which Douglas Shelf Seven Ltd were now seeking to rely. Had they not done so, this too would have been listed in the Minute of Variation for deletion. Therefore the Minute of Variation should be rectified to that effect.

---

1 *Co-operative Wholesale Society Ltd v Ravenseft Properties Ltd* 2003 SCLR 509 at paras [32], [37].
2 2003 SCLR 509.
3 *Co-operative Wholesale Society Ltd v Ravenseft Properties Ltd* 2001 GWD 24-905, discussed in *Conveyancing 2001* pp 121–2; 2002 SCLR 644, discussed in *Conveyancing 2002* pp 99–100.
4 For that reason the earlier stages of the litigation concentrated on s 9 of the Law Reform (Miscellaneous Provisions) (Scotland) Act 1985, the argument being that any rectification would be to the prejudice of Douglas Shelf Seven Ltd as a third party.

The court refused to grant the application. It was plain from the evidence that the parties had intended to delete clause (sixth) and clause (sixth) alone. The Minute of Variation had therefore given proper effect to their common intention. It was true, no doubt, that that intention had been formed to some extent in ignorance. Had they been better informed they might have decided to do otherwise. But it was not the task of the court to give effect to what might, or might not, have been the intention of the parties in circumstances which had not arisen. Section 8 of the Law Reform (Miscellaneous Provisions) (Scotland) Act 1985 was concerned only with the parties' actual intention, and that intention was not, on the evidence, in doubt. In the words of Lord Eassie:[1]

> The power to allow rectification is … a limited one. In my view it is not available to recast an initial agreement in the terms which might have been used had the parties been alert to some particular overlooked factual circumstance.

The Co-op had also a wider argument. The agreement to delete clause (sixth), they argued, was only a particular manifestation of a wider intention to delete all keep-open clauses (including those they might not have known about). That wider intention had not been given effect to by the Minute of Variation. Hence rectification should be allowed. This recalls an argument which found favour in an earlier decision, *Bank of Ireland v Bass Brewers*.[2] It amounts to saying that rectification is available, not merely for error in expression, but also for error in expectation. For here there was no error in expression. The deed used the right words – but with the wrong result. The parties intended the words (the deletion of clause (sixth)) but not the result (the continuing presence of a keep-open clause). In the event, the evidence did not support the argument. Had it done so, it is unclear that the argument would have persuaded the court.

Too little land and the protection of third parties

Even in a circumscribed form, however, there is much that s 8 of the Law Reform (Miscellaneous Provisions) (Scotland) Act 1985 can do. *Jones v Wood*[3] tells a tale of conveyancing disaster, but it was a disaster which s 8 was designed to alleviate.

The owners of a farm divided it into two parts. One part, comprising the farm house, steading and some land, was sold to the pursuers. The rest of the land was sold to someone else. Unfortunately the plans in the dispositions were defective, in that almost an acre was omitted from the pursuers' plan and included instead on the plan attached to the disposition of the farm land. Although the missing acre included buildings, the mistake was not noticed. The pursuer's disposition was granted, and registered, first. In due course a land certificate was issued.

1 *Co-operative Wholesale Society Ltd v Ravenseft Properties Ltd* 2003 SCLR 509 at para [31].
2 *Bank of Ireland v Bass Brewers* 2000 GWD 20-786, 2000 GWD 28-1077, discussed in *Conveyancing 2000* pp 118–9. Surprisingly, this decision does not seem to have been put before the court.
3 *Jones v Wood* (27 October 2003, unreported), Dumfries Sheriff Court. It is understood that the decision has been appealed to the Court of Session.

Naturally enough, the acre was also missing from the title plan. The purchasers of the farm land sold on within a few months to a third party who likewise registered his disposition. The land certificate issued in his favour included the missing acre.

When the mistake was discovered the pursuers sought to put matters right. The third party – now registered as owner of a windfall acre – was unwilling to relinquish his gain. In those circumstances the pursuers raised an action in which they sought (1) rectification of the plan attached to the original disposition in their favour so as to restore the missing acre and, consequentially, (2) rectification of the title sheet of their property to the same effect.[1]

It is worth pausing to consider the consequences in property law of these craves. Rectification – both of the deed[2] and, in this isolated case only,[3] of the Land Register – is retrospective, so that, if granted, the effect is as if the deed and Register had always been in those terms. In many respects this re-writing of history is puzzling and illogical, but in the present case it operated to the pursuers' benefit.[4] For if the missing acre could be added, retrospectively, to the disposition, the result would be to make the subsequent disposition of the farm land, also retrospectively, *a non domino* in respect of the acre. Both title sheets would then be inaccurate, the pursuers' for including too little and the third party's for including too much. The missing acre could be added to the pursuer's title sheet, and removed at the same time from the third party's. Rectification of the Register would be possible in the second case because it was the pursuers, and not the third party, who were in possession and so there could be no question of prejudice to a proprietor in possession.[5]

In principle, the case for rectification of the deed was overwhelming. The missives included the acre. The disposition did not. There was no suggestion that the parties had changed their minds between missives and disposition, and indeed the pursuers had taken, and kept, possession of the acre. The omission in the disposition, in short, was no more than a conveyancing blunder – exactly the sort of mistake which s 8 of the Law Reform (Miscellaneous Provisions) (Scotland) Act 1985 is designed to correct.

There was, however, a complication. The missing acre had not simply been retained by the granter of the deed, as sometimes happens. Instead it had been

---

1 Note that only the first of those is judicial rectification under s 8 of the Law Reform (Miscellaneous Provisions) (Scotland) Act 1985. The second is rectification of the Land Register by the Keeper, under s 9 of the Land Registration (Scotland) Act 1979. That follows as an automatic consequence of rectification of the deed, even in a case where it is to the prejudice of a proprietor in possession: see LR(S)A 1979, s 9(3)(b).

2 LR (MP)(S)A 1985, s 8(4); but see also s 9(4) of the 1985 Act.

3 Rectification of the Land Register is not usually retrospective, but there is a special rule where this follows on from rectification of a deed: see the LR(S)A 1979, s 9(3A).

4 If rectification were not retrospective, it would have been necessary for the pursuers to seek rectification also of the two dispositions of the farm land, because, for as long as they stood, the pursuers' disposition as rectified only prospectively would have been *a non domino* in respect of the missing acre.

5 LR(S)A 1979, s 9(1), (3).

conveyed, along with the farm land, to someone else, and that person had in turn conveyed it to a third party. Third parties, reasonably enough, are protected against rectification, by s 9 of the 1985 Act. Generally speaking, a third party benefits from the s 9 protection if three conditions are met: (1) the third party must have changed his or her position in a material way ('acted or refrained from acting') in reliance on the document in its unrectified form; (2) the third party must have been in good faith, or at any rate the reliance must have been reasonable; and (3) the rectification must be materially prejudicial to the third party.

In the present case there was, as usual, no real difficulty as to the third of these conditions. The precise value of the acre was disputed but was in the region of £10,000. Currently it was the property of the third party. Plainly, its loss would be materially detrimental to his position.

The case turned mainly on the first condition. Had there been reliance? And, if so, had the third party changed his position as a result? On the evidence, the sheriff held that the answer was in the negative in both cases. It is true that the third party's solicitor had examined the pursuers' disposition so that the third party, through his solicitor, could be regarded as familiar with its contents. But, in the sheriff's view, reliance in this context meant not a general acquaintance with the deed but specific reliance on the defectively expressed term itself, or in other words the omission of the acre. No such specific reliance could be shown. The land was being acquired for forestry. The third party had no interest in the missing acre or in the buildings on it, and no reason for noticing their omission. Nor had he changed his position as a result for, on the evidence, he would have bought the land even if the boundaries in the pursuers' disposition had been correctly drawn.

The sheriff's approach to the first condition is much the same as that adopted by Lord Nimmo Smith in a case decided the previous year, *Sheltered Housing Management Ltd v Cairns.*[1] It seems sound in principle. Unless reliance has been specific and focused, there is no reason why rectification should be refused. Yet while the law is perhaps reasonably clear, its application to particular sets of facts will often be difficult. It may be hard to show, after the event, that a third party had specific knowledge of the presence – or, more difficult still, the absence – of one clause out of many. And it may be no less hard to show that that was the reason – or at least a main reason – for proceeding with the transaction.

Title Conditions (Scotland) Act 2003

Introduction

The Title Conditions (Scotland) Act 2003 (asp 9) is closely related to the Abolition of Feudal Tenure etc (Scotland) Act 2000 and, like that Act, is intended to come into force mainly on the 'appointed day', ie the day on which the feudal system

---

1 *Sheltered Housing Management Ltd v Cairns* 2003 SLT 578, discussed in *Conveyancing 2002* pp 97–100.

will be abolished.[1] That day is 28 November 2004.[2] A small number of provisions, however, came into force on 4 April 2003,[3] including a provision abolishing (non-feudal) irritancy and an important provision on reversions under the School Sites Act 1841.[4] Further, most of Part 3 (allowing the creation of new personal real burdens) came into force on 1 November 2003.[5] The Act has already been amended in some minor respects by statutory instrument,[6] and further changes are contained in the Tenements (Scotland) Bill, which was introduced to the Scottish Parliament on 30 January 2004.

The Act is based on the work of the Scottish Law Commission and follows, for the most part, the draft Bill attached to the Commission's *Report on Real Burdens* (Scot Law Com No 181, 2000; available on www.scotlawcom.gov.uk). That *Report* gives a detailed analysis, and justification, of the legislation. The official explanatory notes are also of assistance. Further useful material is undernoted.[7]

Title conditions

The very name of the Title Conditions (Scotland) Act 2003 is unfamiliar. The term *title conditions* is new, although sometimes used in speech. As used in the Act, 'title conditions' means, essentially, (1) real burdens, (2) servitudes and (3) conditions in long leases; but the Act is mainly about real burdens.[8] Its primary purpose is to restate the common law of real burdens in the form of a quasi-code, but with modifications in response to the abolition of the feudal system or where the existing law was uncertain or in need of improvement.[9] The fact that the legislation grows organically out of the existing law makes it easier to understand, but there are many important changes and a great deal of unfamiliar terminology.

Praedial real burdens and personal real burdens

Under the existing, still feudal, law there are two types of real burden. First there are burdens created in, or in association with, a grant in feu. These *feudal burdens*

---

1 Title Conditions (Scotland) Act 2003, s 129(2).
2 Abolition of Feudal Tenure etc (Scotland) Act 2000 (Commencement No 2) (Appointed Day) Order 2003, SSI 2003/456.
3 TC(S)A 2003, s 129(3).
4 TC(S)A 2003, ss 67 and 86 respectively.
5 Title Conditions (Scotland) Act 2003 (Commencement No 1) Order 2003, SSI 2003/454.
6 Title Conditions (Scotland) Act 2003 (Consequential Provisions) Order 2003, SSI 2003/503.
7 K G C Reid *The Abolition of Feudal Tenure in Scotland* (2003) esp Chapters 5 to 7; R Rennie *Land Tenure Reform* (Greens Essential Legislation, 2003); D A Brand, A J M Steven and S Wortley (eds) *Professor McDonald's Conveyancing Manual* (7th edn, 2004) Part 3; J Connolly 'The Title Conditions (Scotland) Act 2003 and Servitudes' (2003) 8 *Scottish Law and Practice Quarterly* 217; A J M Steven 'Implied Enforcement Rights in relation to Real Burdens in terms of the Title Conditions (Scotland) Act 2003' (2003) 71 *Scottish Law Gazette* 146.
8 For a full definition, see the TC(S)A 2003, s 122(1).
9 In moving that the Title Conditions Bill be passed, Jim Wallace, the Deputy First Minister, said that '[i]t is a classic piece of law reform. It has examined the common law with a cool eye. Where the law was sensible and useful, it has been reproduced in the codes that are set out in the Bill's opening sections. Where the law was uncertain, it has been clarified. Where the law was poor, it is being replaced.' See *Scottish Parliament Official Report* 26 February 2003 col 18741.

are enforceable by the superior for the time being against the vassal (or feuar) for the time being. Co-feuars may also have enforcement rights. Secondly, there are burdens created, outside the feudal relationship, by ordinary disposition. Such *non-feudal burdens* behave much like servitudes. Two pieces of land are necessary. As well as the land affected by the burdens – the *burdened property*, in the terminology of the 2003 Act – there must also be land to which the right of enforcement attaches (the *benefited property*). And non-feudal burdens are thus enforceable by the owner for the time being of the benefited property against the owner for the time being of the burdened property. Feudal burdens need a burdened property as well (ie the feu); but there is no physical benefited property.

After 28 November 2004 there will be no more feudal burdens. But to compensate, in part, for their loss, the Title Conditions (Scotland) Act 2003 introduces a completely new type of burden known as the *personal real burden*. The new division can be seen clearly from s 1 of the Act. In the first place there are *praedial real burdens*, as we may call them[1] (ie the old non-feudal burden). And in the second place there are personal real burdens, burdens 'in favour of a person other than by reference to the person's capacity as owner of any land'. A consideration of personal real burdens may be left until later. For present purposes it is only necessary to say that they are restricted both as to content and as to type of holder. Thus whereas under the current law there is something like a 50:50 split between feudal and non-feudal burdens, under the new law almost all real burdens will be praedial rather than personal. In the text that follows, all references are to praedial real burdens unless otherwise stated.

Praedial real burdens and servitudes

Praedial real burdens, as already mentioned, are close in character to (praedial) servitudes. One of the objects of the legislation is to draw a clear line between them. This is done by focusing on the type of obligation which can be imposed under a real burden or servitude. Essentially there are three, namely:

(1) an obligation to do something (eg maintain a roof);

(2) an obligation not to do something (eg carry on trade or business); and

(3) an obligation to allow the benefited owner to enter or otherwise make use of the burdened property.

Almost always, a real burden consists of the first or the second of these, although the third seems also to be competent.[2] Servitudes are usually of the type (3), in

---

1 Though the Title Conditions (Scotland) Act 2003 does not use the term. 'Predial' is an alternative spelling. There is a corresponding distinction between personal servitudes and praedial (or real) servitudes, which is well known throughout the civil law world. See Stair II.7.pr; Erskine II.9.5. 'Praedial' is from the Latin word *praedium* meaning land or an estate. The only personal servitude recognised in Scots law is proper liferent.
2 K G C Reid *The Law of Property in Scotland* (1996) para 391.

which case they are known as positive servitudes; but they may also be of type (2), in which case they are negative servitudes. As matters stand, therefore, there is a theoretical overlap between servitudes and real burdens in respect of type (3) obligations, and a proper overlap in respect of type (2). This can lead to anomalies. A real burden, for example, can only be created by registration. But if the same obligation were constituted as a negative servitude, registration would not be required.[1]

Section 2 of the Title Conditions (Scotland) Act 2003 sets out the new rules. Normally a real burden must consist either of an obligation to do something (in which case it is called an *affirmative burden*) or an obligation not to do something (in which case it is called a *negative burden*). Obligations of the third type must in future be constituted as positive servitudes rather than as real burdens – a change in law rather than in practice. At the same time s 79 of the 2003 Act prohibits the creation of new negative servitudes. Thus in the future the allowable possibilities, corresponding to the three types of obligation mentioned earlier, will be

(1)   negative burdens;

(2)   affirmative burdens; and

(3)   positive servitudes.

Furthermore, the change is drawn back to apply to existing real burdens and servitudes: on 28 November 2004 all negative servitudes are re-born as negative burdens, and all type (3) real burdens as positive servitudes.[2]

To this redistribution of obligations, s 2(3) of the 2003 Act admits a minor exception. In the future a real burden may be created which, for purposes ancillary to an affirmative or negative burden, (1) consists of a right to enter or otherwise make use of property or (2) makes provision for management or administration. Under the new law the first of these would normally have to be constituted as a positive servitude. Section 2(3) allows the right to be created as a real burden where it is ancillary to other real burdens. An example would be a right to enter property for the purpose of carrying out the repairs required by other burdens. The second part of s 2(3) makes clear that management arrangements – owners' associations, rules for decision-making, the appointment of a manager, and the like – can also be constituted as real burdens, as they frequently are under current practice. Burdens covered by s 2(3) are known as *ancillary burdens*. In the proliferation of terminology introduced by the 2003 Act, however, the terms affirmative, negative and ancillary burdens are of limited importance.

---

1   And if, as usual, registration took place, there is no requirement, as with real burdens, that it be against the title of the burdened property, thus ensuring that a person seeking to acquire that property has proper notice of the obligation.

2   Title Conditions (Scotland) Act 2003, ss 80(1), 81.

Community burdens and neighbour burdens

Thus far we have distinguished ordinary 'praedial' real burdens from the newly invented personal real burdens; and we have explained how the dividing line is now to be drawn between real burdens and servitudes. The final classificatory step necessary at this stage is to distinguish *community burdens* from *neighbour burdens*.[1]

The basic idea here is both simple and familiar. In practice real burdens are created mainly in one of two situations. The *first* is where land is being subdivided. Anne sells part of her garden to Brian, retaining the rest. The disposition imposes real burdens. These are neighbour burdens, enforceable by Anne and her successors as owners of the retained land against Brian and his successors as owners of the disponed land. Neighbour burdens are non-reciprocal in character: Brian's land is burdened in favour of Anne's land, but Anne's land is free.

The *second* situation is the development. Developers build and sell 100 houses. The development is subject to a deed of conditions setting out burdens in respect of which the owner of each house has enforcement rights. These are community burdens, and the development is the 'community'. The essential features of community burdens are:[2]

(1)   that real burdens are imposed on a group of properties under a 'common scheme' (ie under identical or broadly equivalent burdens); and

(2)   that the burdens are mutually enforceable, so that each property in the community is at the same time both a burdened and a benefited property.

It is important to realise that the terms apply to existing burdens as well as to new ones. Thus these are just new labels for well-recognised burden types under the current law.

Not absolutely all real burdens fit neatly into one or other of those categories. And it sometimes happens that the same burdens are *both* neighbour burdens and community burdens, as for example when the owner of a rural estate dispones a number of plots subject to uniform burdens, conferring mutual enforcement rights but at the same time retaining a right to enforce for the benefit of the (unburdened) rump of the estate. But these complications may be passed over for present purposes.

Creation

Part 1 of the Title Conditions (Scotland) Act 2003 sets out the life cycle of the real burden, from creation, through interpretation and enforcement, to eventual

---

1   The term 'neighbour burden' is not, however, found in the Title Conditions (Scotland) Act 2003. See Scottish Law Commission *Report on Real Burdens* (Scot Law Com No 181, 2000; available on www.scotlawcom.gov.uk) para 1.9.

2   TC(S)A 2003, s 25. The requirement that there be at least four units is because the default rules in Part 2 of the Act would operate unfairly with smaller communities.

extinction. We begin with creation. Here some rules of the current law are changed by the legislation, but most are left undisturbed. Where changes are made it is usually with the idea of increasing the transparency of the Register, or to make clear the location of enforcement rights. The rules apply only to real burdens created on or after 28 November 2004.[1]

Which deed?

At present real burdens must be created either in a conveyance or in a (statutory) deed of conditions. The legislation liberalises the position by allowing real burdens to be created in any deed whatsoever.[2] In practice, however, it is likely that conveyances and deeds of conditions will continue to dominate, although the latter lose their former statutory basis.[3]

What words?

As under the present law, the full terms of burden must be set out in the four corners of the deed.[4] Absolute compliance is impossible, however, and it appears to be sufficient if a person examining the deed is given reasonable notice of the obligations in question. Extrinsic evidence will then do the rest.[5] The Title Conditions (Scotland) Act 2003 allows extrinsic evidence expressly in the common situation where liability for maintenance is apportioned according to some measure furth of the deed, such as feuduty or rateable value.[6] The 2003 Act also settles a long-standing dispute by validating, with retrospective effect, obligations to defray maintenance and other costs, notwithstanding that the amount due is not specified (as it could not be in practice).[7]

In a departure from the current law, the deed must use the words 'real burden' or alternatively the name of one of the nominate real burdens such as 'community burden'.[8] The idea is to remove doubt as to whether a real burden is intended.

Permissible content

Section 3 of the Title Conditions (Scotland) Act 2003 codifies the rules developed in *Tailors of Aberdeen v Coutts*[9] and subsequent cases.[10] A real burden must be

---

1 Nothing in the Title Conditions (Scotland) Act 2003 impairs the validity of existing real burdens. See TC(S)A 2003, s 119(1).
2 TC(S)A 2003, s 4(1), (2).
3 Section 32 of the Conveyancing (Scotland) Act 1874 and s 17 of the Land Registration (Scotland) Act 1979 - both repealed by the TC(S)A 2003, s 128, Sch 15. Once the restriction as to type of deed is removed, such special statutory provision ceases to be necessary.
4 TC(S)A 2003, s 4(2)(a): the deed 'sets out ... the terms of the prospective real burden'.
5 See eg *Grampian Joint Police Board v Pearson* 2001 SC 772, discussed in *Conveyancing 2001* pp 88–9.
6 TC(S)A 2003, s 5(2).
7 TC(S)A 2003, s 5(1). For the dispute, see *Conveyancing 2002* pp 65–7 and, most recently, *Crampshee v North Lanarkshire Council* 2004 GWD 7-149.
8 TC(S)A 2003, s 4(2)(a), (3).
9 *Tailors of Aberdeen v Coutts* (1840) 1 Rob 296.
10 K G C Reid *The Law of Property in Scotland* (1996) para 391.

praedial, ie must relate both to the burdened and the benefited property, or, in the case of a community burden, to the community itself. The burden must not be repugnant with ownership, or in other words the obligation must not be so severe as to take away fundamental rights of the owner, such as the right to use the property, or manage or dispose of it. The burden must not be contrary to public policy, illegal, or create a monopoly. However, the 2003 Act allows a developer or other person to reserve a right to act as, or to appoint, a manager for the initial years of a development.[1] Technically this is treated as a special type of personal real burden known as a *manager burden*. Under the legislation a manager burden usually expires after five years, but the period is three years in the case of sheltered or retirement housing and thirty years in the case of houses sold by social landlords under the right-to-buy legislation. The period runs from the date of registration of the deed. This provision of the 2003 Act came into force on 4 April 2003[2] and is retrospective. This means not only that it validates manager burdens already created (for their validity was in doubt)[3] but also that it applies to such burdens the five-year limit. It follows that a manager provision in a deed of conditions registered in 1998 or earlier has now ceased to have effect (except in the case of a right-to-buy development).

For community burdens, s 26 of the 2003 Act gives a list, intended to be helpful, of the kind of managerial provisions that might sensibly be included. In drafting community burdens it is also necessary to bear in mind the default rules in ss 28–31. These provide that the owners of a majority[4] of units in a community can:

(1)   appoint a manager;

(2)   confer powers on the manager;

(3)   dismiss the manager;

(4)   instruct maintenance, where community burdens impose an obligation to pay; and

(5)   require, according to a detailed procedure, payment in advance of the projected cost.

These rules are mainly aimed at existing community burdens where no adequate provision is made for management and decision making.[5] But they will apply to new communities / developments except insofar as the community burdens otherwise provide.

---

1   Title Conditions (Scotland) Act 2003, s 63.

2   TC(S)A 2003, s 129(3).

3   *Conveyancing 2000* pp 70–4.

4   In the case of sheltered or retirement housing, the required threshold is sometimes two thirds. See the TC(S)A 2003, s 54(5).

5   In general the TC(S)A 2003 applies to existing burdens as well as to those created after the appointed day: see s 119(10).

Nomination of benefited property

The current law allows a burden to be created without giving any indication of who is to enforce it. The complex, and largely unworkable, rules of implied enforcement rights then come into play. The Title Conditions (Scotland) Act 2003 abolishes implied enforcement rights.[1] In future, a constitutive deed[2] must nominate and identify not only the burdened property (as under current law and practice), but also the benefited property or properties.[3] In the case of community burdens, where all properties are at the same time both benefited and burdened, this resolves into identifying the community[4] – as already happens in deeds of conditions in current practice. For personal real burdens, the person in whose favour the burden is created must be identified.

Dual registration

At the moment a deed creating real burdens need only be registered against the title of the burdened property. That has the merit of ensuring that a person buying that property has notice of the burdens. But unless the burdens also happen to appear on the title of the benefited property, enforcers may have no idea as to their rights. The Title Conditions (Scotland) Act 2003 requires registration against *both* benefited and burdened property.[5] In fact deeds of conditions imposing community burdens already meet this requirement, for to register against the burdened property is also to register against the benefited (each unit in the community being both). But with subdivisions and neighbour burdens, dual registration will be a change in practice.

Date of creation

The default rule is that a real burden becomes live on the date of registration. But in the same way as the effectiveness of a deed of conditions can currently be postponed by excluding s 17 of the Land Registration (Scotland) Act 1979, so under the new law the constitutive deed can make provision for postponed effectiveness.[6]

Identifying the benefited property

Express nomination

Quite often the constitutive deed confers express enforcement rights on the owners of a particular property or properties. In that case the properties in question are the benefited properties.[7] All burdens created after the appointed

---

1 Title Conditions (Scotland) Act 2003, s 49(1).
2 The 'constitutive deed' is the deed in which the real burdens are set out: see TC(S)A 2003, s 122(1).
3 TC(S)A 2003, s 4(2)(c).
4 TC(S)A 2003, s 4(4).
5 TC(S)A 2003, s 4(5).
6 TC(S)A 2003, s 4(1).
7 Strictly, the new rules on implied rights under common schemes etc (TC(S)A 2003, ss 52–57, discussed below) apply even in a case where express enforcement rights are conferred; but in practice the rights implied under these provisions are likely to be identical to those expressed.

day, as already mentioned, must identify the benefited property, and it is highly desirable to do so even before that day. In addition, former feudal burdens converted to neighbour burdens by registration of a notice under s 18 of the Abolition of Feudal Tenure etc (Scotland) Act 2000 must also, in the notice, identify the benefited property.[1]

Implied nomination: common schemes

In the absence of express rights, the position is much more difficult. Under the current law it depends on the, largely unworkable, rules of implied enforcement rights.[2] The Title Conditions (Scotland) Act 2003 changes the law.[3] An initial distinction is made between (1) burdens imposed under a common scheme and (2) other burdens – a distinction which corresponds, more or less, to the distinction made earlier between (community) burdens imposed on a development and (neighbour) burdens imposed on a subdivision.

Where burdens were imposed under a common scheme on *related properties*, s 53 of the 2003 Act provides that each property is a benefited property as well as a burdened property – or in other words, that the burdens are community burdens. Existing, and in practice less extensive, implied rights are abolished.[4] Factors favouring an inference that properties are 'related' for this purpose include the situation where properties are subject to the common scheme by virtue of a deed of conditions, or share a common facility or an obligation of maintenance.[5] In introducing s 53 the Deputy First Minister said that 'houses on a typical housing estate would be related properties' but not 'scattered properties in rural areas'.[6] For s 53 to apply, the deed imposing the burdens must have been registered before the appointed day (or, if imposed by a series of break-off writs, at least one of these must have been so registered).

Section 53 has been attacked as extending enforcement rights too widely, thus making it difficult or impossible to obtain minutes of waiver.[7] The problem is particularly acute in the case of housing estates where, currently, no co-feuars' rights exist, so that only the superior need be approached for a waiver. The effect of s 53 will be to substitute for the superior the owners of the 100 other houses on the estate. But there are also arguments in its favour. Section 53 has the merit of treating all housing estates (and other developments) alike. If burdens are imposed on a common plan, then everyone can enforce them. That is simple and, arguably, fair. At present, the position is patchy, depending on whether the words

1 Abolition of Feudal Tenure etc (Scotland) Act 2000, s 18(2)(b). Dual registration is also required.
2 On those rules see further K G C Reid *The Law of Property in Scotland* (1996) paras 398–404.
3 For a much fuller account than is possible here, see K G C Reid *The Abolition of Feudal Tenure in Scotland* (2003) Chapter 5.
4 Title Conditions (Scotland) Act 2003, s 49(1).
5 TC(S)A 2003, s 53(2).
6 *Scottish Parliament Official Report* (Justice 1 Committee) 10 December 2002 col 4372.
7 In this respect the TC(S)A 2003 is different from the draft produced by the Scottish Law Commission, which would have restricted enforcement rights to neighbours within four metres. See Scottish Law Commission *Report on Real Burdens* (Scot Law Com No 181, 2000) paras 11.48–11.58.

used in the deed happened to be sufficient to confer enforcement rights, itself often a matter of chance. In any case, the difficulty of obtaining waivers already exists on many housing estates and is addressed by the 2003 Act in other ways, by providing alternative methods of discharge.[1]

In addition to s 53 two further sections make provision for enforcement rights in common scheme cases,[2] but both are of limited applicability and will not be considered further here. More important is s 56 which provides that where *facility burdens* are created before the appointed day, the benefited properties are, logically enough, all those which take benefit from the facility in question. Facility burdens – another key term – are real burdens for the maintenance, management, reinstatement or use of facilities (such as the common parts of a tenement or a garden wall or a private road).[3]

Implied nomination: subdivisions

In addition to providing for common schemes, the Title Conditions (Scotland) Act 2003 also makes provision for 'other' cases – in effect for subdivisions occurring before the appointed day. In the example given earlier, Anne dispones part of her garden to Brian. As the law currently stands, it is implied that the part still retained by Anne is the benefited property in any burdens imposed by the disposition.[4] The 2003 Act keeps this rule, but only for ten years.[5] In the meantime Anne must register a notice to preserve her enforcement rights.[6] Failure to do so means that her rights will be lost on 28 November 2014. The only implied rights left after that date will be those created in common scheme cases as already described.

Division of the benefited property

If a benefited property is divided, each separate part retains its status as such. Sometimes the result is an unacceptable proliferation of enforcement rights. This problem of the existing law is tackled by s 12 of the Title Conditions (Scotland) Act 2003. In future, a part split off from the benefited property will not itself be a benefited property unless the disposition provides otherwise. Sometimes it will be sensible so to provide, but in other cases the plots involved will be so small or remote as to make enforcement of the burdens of no interest, whether practically or legally. Section 12 does not apply to community burdens, on the basis that all units in a community should continue to have mutual rights regardless of sub-division.

---

1 Title Conditions (Scotland) Act 2003, ss 32–37, discussed below.
2 TC(S)A 2003, ss 52 (common scheme cases not involving related properties) and 54 (common scheme cases for sheltered and retirement housing).
3 TC(S)A 2003, s 122. For a full discussion, see K G C Reid *The Abolition of Feudal Tenure in Scotland* (2003) Chapter 6.
4 *J A Mactaggart & Co v Harrower* (1906) 8 F 1101. For a discussion, see *Conveyancing 1999* pp 59–61.
5 TC(S)A 2003, s 49(2).
6 TC(S)A 2003, s 50.

Enforcement

Section 8(1) of the 2003 Act, codifying the current law, provides that: 'a real burden is enforceable by any person who has both title and interest to enforce it'.

Survival of burdens

Naturally, only those burdens that survive the appointed day can be enforced. Non-feudal burdens are unaffected by the abolition of the feudal system, and while many feudal burdens will be extinguished,[1] many others will survive, under provisions in the Abolition of Feudal Tenure etc (Scotland) Act 2000 or the Title Conditions (Scotland) Act 2003.[2]

Title

In praedial real burdens, title is tied to the benefited property. At present only the owner of such property has title to enforce. To owners the 2003 Act adds tenants, proper liferenters and spouses with an occupancy right.[3] The idea is that any person with a real right of occupation should be able to enforce burdens created for the benefit of the property, for usually it is the occupier who is most affected by a breach. This entitlement, it should be stressed, has no bearing on discharge. The owner remains the sole holder of the real burdens, and only the owner can grant a minute of waiver. Conversely, there is no need – no purpose indeed – in having a waiver signed by a tenant or by a spouse with an occupancy right.

It need hardly be added that, as of the appointed day, superiors cease to have any right to enforce in their capacity as such, although in some cases enforcement rights will have been preserved by registration of notices under Part 4 of the Abolition of Feudal Tenure etc (Scotland) Act 2000.

Interest

The current rules on interest to enforce are codified.[4] In general there is interest if, in the particular circumstances that have arisen, the breach will result in material detriment to the value or enjoyment of the enforcer's right in the benefited property. Interest must therefore be praedial rather than personal. There is also interest to recover any money that is due. In housing estates and other large developments those who have interest, in respect of a particular breach, will often be a much smaller class than those who have title.

Persons against whom enforceable

All burdens are enforceable against the owner of the burdened property.[5] In addition, negative burdens (ie burdens imposing a restriction) are enforceable

---

1 Abolition of Feudal Tenure etc (Scotland) Act 2000, s 17(1).
2 For a full discussion, see K G C Reid *The Abolition of Feudal Tenure in Scotland* (2003) Chapter 7.
3 Title Conditions (Scotland) Act 2003, s 8(2).
4 TC(S)A 2003, s 8(3).
5 TC(S)A 2003, s 9.

against tenants and other persons having use of the property. This removes a doubt in the existing law, as well as providing a rule which is obviously sensible.

There is a special rule where property changes hands at a time when an affirmative burden (ie an obligation to do something, such as pay money) is outstanding. Both the outgoing and incoming owners are liable, jointly and severally; but, except insofar as is otherwise agreed (eg in missives), an incoming owner who is made to pay can recover from the outgoing owner.[1]

Interpretation

Burdens have tended to be interpreted by the courts in a manner that is over-strict with the result, sometimes, that the burden is treated as void or fails to achieve the effect which was plainly intended.[2] Section 14 of the Title Conditions (Scotland) Act 2003 attempts to restore the balance by providing that:

> Real burdens shall be construed in the same manner as other provisions of deeds which relate to land and are intended for registration.

The effect should be to bring real burdens into line with, for example, servitudes, leases and standard securities.

Remedies

One existing remedy is removed altogether by the legislation. Irritancy was commonly provided for in grants of feu but only infrequently in ordinary dispositions, where indeed its validity was open to question. Irritancy for feudal real burdens was abolished on 9 June 2000 by the Abolition of Feudal Tenure etc (Scotland) Act 2000.[3] The Title Conditions (Scotland) Act 2003 now abolishes non-feudal irritancies with effect from 4 April 2003.[4]

Extinction by discharge

It is in the area of extinction that the most important changes made by the Title Conditions (Scotland) Act 2003 occur. An initial distinction falls to be made between extinction by discharge and extinction by breach. We begin with the first of those.

---

1 Title Conditions (Scotland) Act 2003, s 10.
2 K G C Reid *The Law of Property in Scotland* (1996) paras 415–422. For recent examples, see *Heritage Fisheries Ltd v Duke of Roxburghe* 2000 SLT 800; *Grampian Joint Police Board v Pearson* 2001 SC 772.
3 Abolition of Feudal Tenure etc (Scotland) Act 2000, ss 53, 77.
4 TC(S)A 2003, ss 67, 129(3).

Minute of waiver

The ordinary minute of waiver will of course continue to be available. And the Title Conditions (Scotland) Act 2003 makes clear what was previously in doubt, namely that a completed title is not necessary in order to grant such a deed provided, in Sasine cases, there is deduction of title.[1] As already mentioned, the fact that tenants and others can now enforce burdens has no bearing on minutes of waiver which, as before, need be granted only by the owner.

From the conveyancer's point of view, one of the great conveniences of the feudal system was that a single person could grant a minute of waiver. True, the superior might exact a price; but the whole transaction could usually be carried out quickly and painlessly. Of course superiors' waivers were relied on more than was entirely proper. There was a natural tendency to overlook co-feuars' rights and hence the fact that, where such rights existed, a waiver from the superior was of little value. But, for better or for worse, many transactions were settled on the basis of a deed signed by the superior alone. This convenient device will disappear on 28 November 2004. Instead it will be necessary to focus much more carefully than in the past on the location of enforcement rights. The effect of the 2003 Act is that the answer will be readily discoverable in most cases, but quite often, to conveyancers at least, the answer will be unwelcome. In particular, as already mentioned, if the property is part of a housing estate or other development, the effect of s 53 is usually to confer enforcement rights on everyone in the estate. At this point any idea of a minute of waiver has to be abandoned.

Variation or discharge of community burdens

Partly to meet the difficulty just mentioned, the Title Conditions (Scotland) Act 2003 introduces no fewer than four additional methods of variation or discharge which are available for community burdens only. These are for registration, against the properties affected, of a deed granted by:

(1)   the owners of a majority of units in the community;[2]

(2)   the manager of the community, if duly authorised to do so (whether in the constitutive deed or by a majority of owners under s 28(1)(b));[3]

(3)   such owners as may be specified in the constitutive deed;[4] or

(4)   the owners of the affected unit (or units) together with the owners of all other units in the community within four metres[5] (discounting roads less than 20 metres wide).[6]

---

1   Title Conditions (Scotland) Act 2003, ss 15, 60(1), 123(1).
2   TC(S)A 2003, s 33(2)(a).
3   TC(S)A 2003, s 33(2)(b).
4   TC(S)A 2003, s 33(1)(a).
5   TC(S)A 2003, ss 32, 35(1).
6   TC(S)A 2003, ss 35, 125.

'Variation' includes the imposition of new community burdens.[1] It will be seen that these methods depart, on one view radically, from the principle of variation and discharge by the owners of *all* the benefited properties.

The method adopted in any particular case is likely to depend both on the size of the community and on whether the discharge is for one unit only or for all (or most) of the units. Most discharges are in respect of only a single unit. In that case the easiest method will usually be the final one (four-metre discharge), as requiring the smallest number of signatories. Only if the community is small are the other methods likely to be attractive. The four-metre rule matches the rules of neighbour notification for the purposes of planning permission,[2] and it may be that the two processes could be combined. The four-metre discharge is not, however, available for facility burdens (ie those concerned with the management or maintenance of a shared facility) or in one or two other cases.[3]

If the discharge is for all units, one of the other methods is likely to be selected, and often only the first will be available in practice. Here again much depends on the size of the community. In an estate of 20 or even 30 houses, obtaining the signatures of a majority of owners may be a reasonable proposition. For much larger numbers the task is likely to be unachievable.

In practice deeds of conditions do not at the moment contain provisions as to how deeds of variation or discharge are to be signed, and so there is nothing to trigger the third method described above. But there is much to be said for changing drafting practice with immediate effect, in anticipation of the coming into force of the legislation. So, for example, in a large housing estate it might be provided that a discharge can be granted by a relatively low percentage of owners, such as 20% or even less. Or immediate neighbours might be given the right, at least in respect of discharges affecting only one unit. Or a more complex scheme might be adopted, whereby certain core burdens required a higher percentage than other, less important, burdens. Provision may only be made for discharge by *owners*, or by the manager acting on their behalf. The Title Conditions (Scotland) Act 2003 expressly prohibits a provision 'to the effect that a person other than the holder of the burden may waive compliance with, or mitigate, or otherwise vary, a condition of the burden'.[4] Thus it would not be possible for developers to reserve to themselves the right to discharge the burdens, in the manner formerly achievable by means of the feudal system.

Obtaining the necessary signatures is not the only step. Those who have not signed stand to lose their rights without their consent. Therefore they must be informed, and given the opportunity to object.[5] Usually this involves sending a

---

1 Title Conditions (Scotland) Act 2003, ss 33(1), 122(1).
2 For a discussion, see Scottish Law Commission *Report on Real Burdens* (Scot Law Com No 181, 2000) paras 11.50 and 11.51.
3 Service burdens and in sheltered or retirement housing. See the Title Conditions (Scotland) Act 2003, s 35(1)(b).
4 TC(S)A 2003, s 3(8).
5 TC(S)A 2003, ss 34, 36, 37(1).

copy of the executed deed together with a notice and explanatory note in statutory form. In the case, however, of four-metre discharges it is sufficient to fix a notice to the affected property and to an appropriate lamp post or posts – presumably on the basis that those most directly affected have already indicated their consent by signature.[1] Once notice has been given, any owner who did not sign may apply to the Lands Tribunal within eight weeks for preservation, unvaried, of the burden insofar as constituted against the units whose owners (or all of whose owners) did not sign. The application then proceeds much in the same way as an ordinary Lands Tribunal case except that the applicant is the benefited owner and not the burdened.[2]

Although the deed can be registered at once, it would not then vary or discharge the burdens in respect of the properties whose owners have not signed. So in practice there is a delay of eight weeks to allow for applications to the Lands Tribunal. Assuming that none is received the Tribunal will endorse the deed with a statement to that effect.[3] In addition the grantee (or one of them) must swear or affirm before a notary public, with an appropriate endorsement on the deed, that intimation duly took place and as to the date when the eight-week period expired.[4] The deed is now ready for registration, and on registration the burdens are duly discharged, or varied.

The procedure is, necessarily, cumbersome and slow. It will be useful for relatively small communities, or in relation to discharges for single units. Even then it is likely to take several months, to involve, possibly significant, expense, and to run the risk of neighbours who refuse to sign or cannot readily be traced. But in the context, for example, of building operations requiring planning permission, the additional hurdle of a four-metre discharge does not seem unacceptably onerous.

Sunset rule

If the burdens are more than 100 years old, there is a faster and more streamlined procedure. Furthermore, it is not confined to community burdens, although facility burdens and a handful of other burden types are excluded.[5] In operation it resembles the four-metre discharge described above, except that the privilege of those owners within four metres is merely to receive an actual copy of the notice proposing the termination of the burdens.

In outline the procedure is as follows.[6] The owner of the burdened property – or any other person, such as a tenant, against whom the burden in question is

---

1 Title Conditions (Scotland) Act 2003, s 36(2). If there are no lamp posts, it is permissible to intimate by newspaper advertisement.
2 TC(S)A 2003, ss 90(1)(c), 97, 98.
3 TC(S)A 2003, ss 34(4), 37(2), (3).
4 TC(S)A 2003, ss 34(4), 37(4).
5 TC(S)A 2003, s 20(3). The others include conservation burdens, maritime burdens and service burdens.
6 TC(S)A 2003, ss 20–24.

enforceable – draws up a notice of termination in statutory form. The notice is sent to the owners of all benefited properties within four metres. In respect of other benefited properties it is sufficient to fix a notice on the burdened property and on an appropriate lamp post or posts. Benefited owners then have a minimum period of eight weeks to object by applying to the Lands Tribunal for renewal of the burden.[1] If no application is made (or if it does not extend to all the burdens, or all the benefited properties), the notice is endorsed with a certificate by the Tribunal and may then be registered. On registration the burden is extinguished (subject to the outcome of any Tribunal application) – or, in the metaphor of the name by which the rule has come to be known, the sun sets on the burden.

The sunset rule is a quick and convenient way of removing awkward burdens in times of need, such as when property is being sold and a breach comes to light. But it would also be open to use at any time to bring to an end any burdens more than 100 years old; and a single notice can be used for all burdens falling into this category.[2] Whether the result will be an irresistible urge to cleanse one's title remains to be seen. It is conceivable that missives will routinely require of the seller that a notice of termination is duly served and registered.

Variation or discharge by the Lands Tribunal

The familiar jurisdiction of the Lands Tribunal remains in place, subject to some changes designed to streamline and speed up the procedure.[3] In particular, if an application is unopposed, the Tribunal is no longer required to consider its merits but must grant the application.[4] A person wishing to oppose an application must now pay a fee,[5] and may be liable for expenses if unsuccessful.[6] The grounds on which an application may be granted, in opposed cases, are reconfigured and extended, but with only limited change in substance.[7] The Tribunal is given a new jurisdiction to pronounce on the validity of real burdens, and on their enforceability and construction.[8] The overall result should be to make a Tribunal application a swifter and, it may be, a cheaper option than at present. Even now conveyancers tend to underestimate its value. As before, the Lands Tribunal is available, not only for real burdens, but for other title conditions as well, most notably for servitudes and conditions in long leases.

---

1 Title Conditions (Scotland) Act 2003, s 90(1)(b)(i).
2 TC(S)A 2003, s 20(6).
3 See generally Part 9 of the Title Conditions (Scotland) Act 2003. The current legislation, which is being replaced, is contained in the Conveyancing and Feudal Reform (Scotland) Act 1970, ss 1, 2.
4 TC(S)A 2003, s 97. This applies only to real burdens, and even then excludes facility burdens, service burdens, and community burdens in sheltered or retirement housing.
5 TC(S)A 2003, s 96(2).
6 TC(S)A 2003, s 103.
7 TC(S)A 2003, s 100.
8 TC(S)A 2003, s 90(1)(a)(ii).

Section 92 of the Title Conditions (Scotland) Act 2003 allows constitutive deeds to carry a provision preventing Lands Tribunal applications for up to five years from the date of creation.

Compulsory purchase

It is usually assumed that compulsory purchase extinguishes all real burdens and servitudes, although the authorities are less clear than one might wish.[1] The Title Conditions (Scotland) Act 2003 removes any doubt. From 1 November 2003 all real burdens and servitudes are extinguished on registration of a conveyance following a compulsory purchase order except insofar as the conveyance or order otherwise provides.[2] The rule does not insist on a so-called statutory conveyance[3] but applies even in the case of ordinary dispositions; and indeed there seems little point in using statutory conveyances in the future.

A slightly different rule applies to acquisitions by agreement, in the shadow of the statutory powers.[4] Here the acquiring authority must first give notice – typically by advertisement or by fixing a notice to the property and an appropriate lamp post – to the owners of any benefited property. There is then a period of not less then 21 days during which such an owner may apply to the Lands Tribunal for renewal of the condition.[5] The procedure is much as already described in the context of the sunset rule and the discharge of community burdens. Assuming that no application is received, a certificate to that effect is endorsed on the conveyance by the Lands Tribunal. Following registration, all real burdens and servitudes are extinguished.

Extinction by breach

Quite often no discharge is sought, either because the burdened owner does not know of the burden, or because the owner knows but decides to take a chance. If the infringement is slight and the cost and trouble of a formal discharge disproportionately high, the temptation to take a chance may be irresistible. Usually it will pay off, for if the burden is not insisted on at the time of breach, the chance to enforce it may be lost forever. This is because, depending on the circumstances, the burden is extinguished by the breach. That may come about in more than one way.

---

1 Scottish Law Commission *Report on Real Burdens* (Scot Law Com No 181, 2000) para 13.14.
2 Title Conditions (Scotland) Act 2003, s 106. For commencement, see the TC(S)A 2003 (Commencement No 1) Order 2003, SSI 2003/454.
3 Ie a conveyance in the form of Sch A to the Lands Clauses Consolidation (Scotland) Act 1845.
4 TC(S)A 2003, s 107.
5 TC(S)A 2003, ss 90(1)(b)(ii), 107(5).

Negative prescription

The period of negative prescription is reduced by the Title Conditions (Scotland) Act 2003 from 20 years to five.[1] In effect, this means that any breach of more than five years ceases to be challengeable and can be disregarded. Normally the five years run from the date of the breach but, to avoid retrospective change, for pre-appointed day breaches the five years run from the appointed day.[2] The usual rules about interruption of prescription apply. Once the prescriptive period has run the burden is extinguished, but only to the extent of the breach. Thus for example if, in breach of an obligation not to build, a garage is erected, the burden is, at the end of five years, extinguished with respect to the garage but not otherwise. Further buildings would be unlawful.

Acquiescence

Section 16 is one of the most important provisions of the Title Conditions (Scotland) Act 2003, and is intended to make acquiescence of much greater practical help than under the present law.[3] The provision applies wherever a real burden is breached in such a way that material expenditure is incurred, the benefit of which would be substantially lost if the burden were now to be enforced. In practice this will usually involve cases of unauthorised building. Section 16 provides that the burden is extinguished to the extent of the breach if either the owner of the benefited property consented to the work, however informally, or where all those with enforcement rights (which might include tenants and other occupiers) either consented or failed to object within the period ending 12 weeks after the work is substantially completed (or a shorter period if that is reasonable).[4] The work must be sufficiently obvious that the enforcers knew, or ought to have known, of it. In effect, enforcers must object at once or lose their rights. For the purposes of the provision a person with a title to enforce but, in the context of the particular breach, no interest, is disregarded.[5]

Perhaps even more important is what happens afterwards. Once the 12-week period has expired, s 16 of the 2003 Act creates a presumption, unless the contrary can be shown, that no objection was made and hence that the burden was duly extinguished. This has implications for unauthorised alterations discovered in the course of a conveyancing transaction. If the alteration is

---

1 Title Conditions (Scotland) Act 2003, s 18.
2 TC(S)A 2003, s 18(5), (6). The former 20-year period can also be used, so that a breach which occurred 17 years before the appointed day would be extinguished 3 years (and not 5 years) after that day.
3 It is assumed, however, that the common law of acquiescence survives to the extent that it is not replaced by s 16 of the TC(S)A 2003.
4 The ground of failure to object does not, however, apply to conservation burdens, economic development burdens or health care burdens.
5 For absence of interest to enforce, see the TC(S)A 2003, s 17, discussed below.

obviously old, then the breach can be taken to have been cured by negative prescription, now reduced to five years. If the alteration is more recent, the presumption in s 16 may usually be accepted as sufficient to deal with the problem. Conveyancers, if they are wise, will not insist on a minute of waiver – even assuming that, in practical terms, one were potentially available. For it is most unlikely that the statutory presumption would be overcome, and even if it were it is difficult to see what the enforcer could do after a lapse of time. Irritancy is no longer available. It is too late for interdict. Damages are due only if the enforcer can show loss, which in most cases would not be possible. And while an enforcer might seek a court order to have the work undone, courts are in practice, and for obvious reasons, reluctant to order the demolition of a building.[1] No doubt some circumstances would remain where a waiver, or Lands Tribunal application, would be prudent. But in the standard case it is unlikely to be needed.

Absence of interest to enforce

It sometimes happens that a particular breach is too slight, or remote, for anyone to have an interest to enforce. In that case, s 17 of the Title Conditions (Scotland) Act 2003 provides that the burden is extinguished to the extent of the breach.

Personal real burdens

In general

After the appointed day, the overwhelming majority of real burdens will be praedial burdens. But there will also be a number of personal real burdens. This is a new category, created for the benefit of various, mainly public, bodies.[2] In a sense the personal real burden is the successor of the old feudal burden, allowing a body to sell its only property in a particular area (so that there is no question of a neighbour burden) and yet still impose real burdens. But compared to the universal availability of feudal burdens, the personal real burden is severely restricted. Only certain bodies qualify, and then only in respect of burdens imposed for certain purposes.

The dissonance in the name is deliberate. A personal real burden is, in a sense, both personal and real. It is personal in respect that it is constituted in favour of a person without reference to land. There is no benefited property. But it is real in respect that it affects land and so is, in the strict sense, a real right. Indeed, viewed more broadly, personal real burdens are actually *typical* real rights – rights held by a person in a thing – while it is praedial burdens that are unusual in insisting on a benefited property.[3]

---

1 K G C Reid *The Law of Property in Scotland* (1996) para 423.
2 Uniquely, manager burdens are not restricted as to holder.
3 Unusual but not unique. Servitudes also need a benefited property (dominant tenement).

The main provisions for personal real burdens are found in Part 3 of the Title Conditions (Scotland) Act 2003, which came into force on 1 November 2003 and allowed the creation of new burdens from that date.[1] Burdens which have already been created as feudal burdens but which would otherwise qualify as personal real burdens may be converted into personal real burdens by registration by the superior, before the appointed day, of a notice in the appropriate statutory form. The conversion then takes effect on the appointed day itself.[2] Thus, at least initially, most personal real burdens will be former feudal burdens converted under this procedure.

The body holding a personal real burden is presumed to have interest to enforce, and in practice the presumption will be difficult to overturn.[3] Some personal real burdens are assignable while others are not.[4] An assignee can enforce a burden even without completing title.[5] Provision is made by the 2003 Act for completion of title and for minutes of waiver.[6] But for the most part personal real burdens are subject to the same rules as praedial real burdens.

It seems useful to list, and briefly explain, the different types of personal real burden. The Scottish Law Commission recommended only two such burdens (conservation burdens and maritime burdens),[7] but the number has now increased to eight.

Conservation burdens

Only conservation bodies, and Scottish Ministers, can hold conservation burdens. Conservation bodies are prescribed by statutory instrument and include all local authorities as well as a number of other bodies, both public and private.[8] Conservation burdens must have the purpose of preserving or protecting, for the benefit of the public, the architectural or historical features of land or other special characteristics such as flora, fauna or general appearance.[9] A typical use would be where a private conservation trust restores

---

1 Other than s 43 of the Title Conditions (Scotland) Act 2003. See the Title Conditions (Scotland) Act 2003 (Commencement No 1) Order 2003, SSI 2003/454.
2 Abolition of Feudal Tenure etc (Scotland) Act 2000, ss 18A, 18B, 18C, 27, 27A. For a full discussion, see K G C Reid *The Abolition of Feudal Tenure in Scotland* (2003) Chapter 4.
3 TC(S)A 2003, s 47.
4 The assignable burdens are personal pre-emption burdens, personal redemption burdens, conservation burdens, rural housing burdens and manager burdens: see the Abolition of Feudal Tenure etc (Scotland) Act 2000, s 18B(7), and the TC(S)A 2003, ss 39, 43(10), 63(3). The others cannot be assigned: see TC(S)A 2003, ss 44(2), 45(4)(b), 46(4(b).
5 TC(S)A 2003, s 40.
6 TC(S)A 2003, ss 41, 48.
7 Scottish Law Commission *Report on Real Burdens* (Scot Law Com No 181, 2000) Part 9.
8 See the Title Conditions (Scotland) Act 2003 (Conservation Bodies) Order 2003, SSI 2003/453 (as amended by the Title Conditions (Scotland) Act 2003 (Conservation Bodies) Amendment Order 2003, SSI 2003/621). The complete list is given on p 33 above.
9 TC(S)A 2003, s 38(1).

a house and sells it subject to restrictions designed to preserve its historical character.

Maritime burdens

These are burdens in favour of the Crown in which the burdened property is the foreshore or seabed. A maritime burden must confer public benefit.[1]

Personal pre-emption/redemption burdens

A feudal right of pre-emption (or redemption) can be converted into a personal pre-emption (or redemption) burden if the superior registers an appropriate notice before the appointed day.[2] Except in the case of rural housing burdens, mentioned below, there is no provision in the Title Conditions (Scotland) Act 2003 for personal pre-emption (or redemption) burdens to be created of new. This category, therefore, will be transient in nature.

Rural housing burdens

A right of pre-emption can be created in favour of a designated rural housing body.[3] The purpose, according to the Deputy First Minister, is that 'bodies that sell land in the interests of providing local community housing at affordable prices should be allowed to control the subsequent sale of the land'.[4]

Manager burdens

These have already been mentioned.[5] A manager burden reserves to a developer or any other person a right to act as, or to appoint, a manager of a development. Normally its life is restricted to five years.[6]

Economic development burdens

Local authorities and Scottish Ministers can create, and hold, economic development burdens.[7] There is an obvious difficulty with the idea that a burden which restricts the use to which land is put could be treated as 'promoting economic development', as the legislation requires. But if the restriction is the counterpart of a reduced price, then it is arguable that economic development is promoted. Further, a restriction on one piece of land

---

1 Title Conditions (Scotland) Act 2003, s 44.
2 Abolition of Feudal Tenure etc (Scotland) Act 2000, s 18A.
3 TC(S)A 2003, s 43. This provision is not yet in force.
4 *Scottish Parliament Official Report* 26 February 2003 col 18691.
5 At p 112.
6 TC(S)A 2003, s 63. Strictly, a manager burden could also be created as a neighbour burden, but the same rules as to duration would apply.
7 TC(S)A 2003, s 45.

might have the effect of promoting the economic development of another.[1] Economic development burdens are the equivalent for local authorities of the statutory agreements available for Scottish Enterprise and Highlands and Islands Enterprise.[2]

Health care burdens

Rather similar are health care burdens. These can be held by Scottish Ministers or, until their expected dissolution, by NHS trusts.[3] The burden must have the purpose of promoting the provision of facilities for health care, including ancillary facilities such as accommodation for staff.[4]

Clawback

As the law currently stands, the role of real burdens in securing clawback of development gain can only be a subsidiary one. A direct obligation on the disponee to make a payment in the event of a grant of planning permission would fail as a real burden because it is insufficiently praedial.[5] The new law is the same. Section 3 of the Title Conditions (Scotland) Act 2003 provides that:

(1) A real burden must relate in some way to the burdened property.

(2) The relationship may be direct or indirect but shall not merely be that the obligated person is the owner of the burdened property.

A bare obligation to make payment seems unrelated to the land other than in the sense disallowed by s 3(2).

A real burden can, however, continue to have a supporting role, for example by restricting the land to non-commercial uses. This means that if planning permission is obtained, the owner will still have to negotiate with the burden holder. But unless the seller has retained land which can act as a benefited property (and so create a neighbour burden) even this, limited, use of real burdens will not be available in the future. Local authorities, NHS trusts, and Scottish Ministers, however, will be able to use economic development burdens or health care

---

1 It may be significant in this connection that, in introducing the provision, the Deputy First Minister explained that '[l]ocal authorities will be able to create economic development burdens in circumstances in which they wish to sell land with a view to encouraging economic development *within their area.'* See *Scottish Parliament Official Report* (Justice 1 Committee) 10 December 2002 col 4355.

2 Enterprise and New Towns (Scotland) Act 1990, s 32. Some difficulties with this provision are removed by the Title Conditions (Scotland) Act 2003, s 113. See Scottish Law Commission *Report on Real Burdens* (Scot Law Com No 181, 2000) para 9.38.

3 NHS trusts are to be dissolved by the National Health Service Reform (Scotland) Bill, s 1, currently before the Scottish Parliament. An appropriate amendment is made to the TC(S)A 2003, s 46.

4 TC(S)A 2003, s 46.

5 Scottish Law Commission *Report on Abolition of the Feudal System* (Scot Law Com No 168, 1999) (available on www.scotlawcom.gov.uk) para 5.23.

burdens, and in both cases the praedial rule is overridden[1] to allow a direct obligation to pay money.[2]

In the future, as in the past, the main means of securing clawback will be by standard security, and here the 2003 Act provides some modest help. If, following the registration of a clawback standard security, a s 13 notice[3] was served in respect of a second security, there was an argument that the second security ranked first, on the basis that the sum contingently due under clawback would be a new, and so postponed, 'advance'.[4] The 2003 Act amends s 13 of the Conveyancing and Feudal Reform (Scotland) Act 1970 with effect from 4 April 2003 by substituting 'debt' for 'advances', and so ensures that the clawback security has first ranking.[5]

Development Management Scheme

Part 6 of the Title Conditions (Scotland) Act 2003 introduces a Development Management Scheme as a model scheme, variable in most respects, which is suitable for large developments. The development is to be managed by a residents' association, acting through a manager. Detailed provision is made in respect of powers, meetings, annual budgets, service charges and so on. The Scheme itself, however, is missing from the 2003 Act, as are a number of supporting provisions, and will be added later by an order made by the UK Government under s 104 of the Scotland Act 1998. The reason for the two-stage introduction is that the residents' association is, on one view, a business association and hence involves an area of law which is reserved to Westminster.[6] It may be assumed that the Scheme will follow closely, or even exactly, that set out in Schedule 3 to the draft Bill included in the Scottish Law Commission's *Report on Real Burdens* (Scot Law Com No 181, 2000). Once the relevant provisions have been enacted and are in force, the Scheme will provide an attractive alternative to proceeding, in the traditional way, by deed of conditions and real burdens.

Pre-emptions

Pre-emptions constituted as real burdens fall into two categories. The first, comprising all feudal pre-emptions together with non-feudal pre-emptions created

---

1 Though not expressly: it is not stated that s 3(1), (2) is subject to ss 45(3) and 46(3) of the Title Conditions (Scotland) Act 2003.

2 TC(S)A 2003, ss 45(3), 46(3). The Scottish Law Commission's view, however, was that '[i]n the context of clawback, real burdens are neither appropriate nor are they efficient'. See *Report on Real Burdens* (Scot Law Com No 181, 2000) para 9.34. The efficiency problem is the risk of discharge by the Lands Tribunal. See *Cumbernauld Development Corporation v County Properties and Developments Ltd* 1996 SLT 1106.

3 Ie a notice served under s 13 of the Conveyancing and Feudal Reform (Scotland) Act 1970.

4 Scottish Law Commission *Report on Real Burdens* (Scot Law Com No 181, 2000) paras 9.32 and 9.36.

5 TC(S)A 2003, s 111.

6 Scotland Act 1998, Sch 5, Part II, head C1 (business associations).

after 1 September 1974, are extinguished on the first occasion the property is offered back to the pre-emption holder.[1] The second category, comprising all remaining pre-emptions, are perpetual, so that the property must be offered back each time it is sold. The Title Conditions (Scotland) Act 2003 follows the existing legislation by dealing only with pre-emptions in the first category.[2]

The current rules about offering back are clarified and simplified.[3] In addition, the possibility of a pre-sale undertaking is introduced.[4] The idea is that the pre-emption holder should sign an undertaking not to exercise the pre-emption for a stipulated period. If, during that period, the property is then sold and the disposition registered, the pre-emption is extinguished without it being necessary to offer the property back. Undertakings can be limited by conditions, so that pre-emption holders might, for example, include a threshold price below which they would reserve a right to buy the property.

School Sites Act 1841

Under the School Sites Act 1841 owners were able to convey land (including entailed land) for the building of schools and schoolhouses. Originally these grants were to private trustees, but in due course title passed, first to education boards and ultimately to local authorities. Many of these schools and schoolhouses have now closed and the site sold by local authorities. And typically such sales disregard the third proviso to s 2 of the 1841 Act, which is to the effect that, on the land ceasing to be used for the statutory purposes, it 'shall thereupon immediately revert to and become a portion of the said estate'. For a long time, indeed, this proviso was forgotten about, but in recent years there has been a spate of claims by those entitled, or allegedly entitled, to the reversion. In a case where the site has been sold, this presents a threat to the title of the acquirer.

The Title Conditions (Scotland) Act 2003 contains a provision designed to secure the acquirer's title and, more generally, to regulate the making of claims under the statutory reversion.[5] This came into force on 4 April 2003 and applies to all claims under the School Sites Act except where the reverter has already completed title to the site or otherwise made a binding arrangement with the local authority.[6] The details are complex but in essence the reverter is given the choice of a conveyance of the site or payment of a sum representing its value. If, however, the choice is for a conveyance, the local authority can insist on compensation. Where the trigger event for the reversion occurred after 4 April

---

1 Conveyancing (Scotland) Act 1938, s 9.
2 Title Conditions (Scotland) Act 2003, s 82.
3 TC(S)A 2003, s 84.
4 TC(S)A 2003, s 83.
5 TC(S)A 2003, s 86.
6 TC(S)A 2003, s 86(1), (9).

2003, the reverter is denied the benefit of improvements made to the land and, in the case of a reconveyance, must pay a sum representing their value.

The provision leaves open the question of entitlement to the reversion. Here the law has yet to make a definitive choice as to whether the reversion is personal to the original granter and so passes to the granter's heirs, or whether it is praedial and attaches to the estate from which the land was originally taken.[1] A practical difficulty with the second view is that the original estate may have been broken up. In England and Wales, where the 1841 Act also applies, the reversion is treated as personal.[2]

Servitudes

The abolition of negative servitudes, and the realignment of the boundary between servitudes and real burdens, was mentioned earlier.[3] The Title Conditions (Scotland) Act 2003 makes three other changes of note in respect of servitudes.

Dual registration

At present there is no requirement that a deed creating a servitude be registered, and, if registered, that the registration (as for real burdens) be against the burdened property.[4] Following the new rules for real burdens, the 2003 Act introduces a requirement for servitudes of registration against *both* the benefited and the burdened properties.[5] There is an exception, on practical grounds, for pipeline servitudes.[6] Discharges must also be registered, although only against the burdened property.[7] As before, it remains possible to create servitudes by prescription, in which case nothing will appear on the Register.

Abandonment of the fixed list

At the moment there is a fixed, and short, list of permissible servitudes which has remained more or less unchanged since the eighteenth century.[8] Rights not appearing there cannot be created as servitudes. Section 76 of the Title Conditions (Scotland) Act 2003 abandons this list in the case of servitudes

---

1 Scottish Law Commission *Report on Real Burdens* (Scot Law Com No 181, 2000) para 10.47.
2 *Fraser v Canterbury Diocesan Board of Finance* [2000] Ch 669; *Bath and Wells Diocesan Board of Finance v Jenkinson* [2002] 3 WLR 202.
3 See p 109.
4 *Balfour v Kinsey* 1987 SLT 144. As for real burdens, the Title Conditions (Scotland) Act 2003 uses 'benefited property' and 'burdened property' rather than the tradition 'dominant tenement' and 'servient tenement'.
5 TC(S)A 2003, s 75(1).
6 TC(S)A 2003, s 75(3).
7 TC(S)A 2003, s 78. The Keeper is empowered to make a matching entry in the title sheet of the benefited property: see TC(S)A 2003, s 105; Land Registration (Scotland) Act 1979, s 5(1).
8 D J Cusine and R R M Paisley *Servitudes and Rights of Way* (1998) Chapter 3.

constituted by registration (only). This does not open the floodgates, however. For a right to be recognised it must still comply with the essential characteristics of a positive servitude, such as that it involves limited use of the burdened property, and that it is for the praedial benefit of the benefited property.[1] Following the rule for real burdens,[2] s 76 provides that the right must not be 'repugnant with ownership', that it must not, in other words, be so extensive as to take away the proprietorial rights of the burdened owner. The overall result will be to admit rights about which doubt is usually expressed, such as the right of parking[3] or the right to place a ladder or scaffolding for repairs; but it seems unlikely to lead to a rush of novel servitudes.

The fixed list remains in place for servitudes created by prescription. This is to protect acquirers of the burdened property. An acquirer has, in practice, no notice of such servitudes and a restriction as to type reduces the risk of unexpected encumbrances.

Retrospective validity of pipeline servitudes

Although aqueduct – and hence, probably, a more general right to lead a pipeline – is included in the current list of servitudes, doubt has sometimes been expressed in relation to cables, wires, and other service media. In one case it was held, by a sheriff principal, that the right to lead electricity by overhead cable is not a recognised servitude.[4] The doubts, such as they are, are stilled by s 77 of the Title Conditions (Scotland) Act 2003 which allows, with retrospective effect, a servitude of leading 'a pipe, cable, wire or other such enclosed unit over or under land for any purpose'.

Land Reform (Scotland) Act 2003[5]

Introduction

Land reform was one of the flagship policies of the first Scottish Executive following the devolution settlement in 1999.[6] The Executive saw a need to enshrine in statute access rights to land, as well as to give rural and crofting communities a right to purchase the land upon which they live and work. To give

---

1 *Servitudes and Rights of Way* para 2.01.
2 Title Conditions (Scotland) Act 2003, s 3(6).
3 For which see *Moncreiffe v Jamieson* (2003, unreported), Lerwick Sheriff Court, discussed at pp 68.
4 *Neill v Scobbie* 1993 GWD 13-887.
5 This part is contributed by Andrew J M Steven and Alan Barr, both of the University of Edinburgh. They acknowledge the assistance of Hew Dalrymple, Dominic Harrison, David Houldsworth, Adele Nicol, Randall Nicoll and Christine O'Neill, all of Brodies; John Glover of the Registers of Scotland; and Scott Wortley of the University of Strathclyde.
6 In this connection, see the relevant pages on the Scottish Executive's website: www.scotland.gov.uk/landreform.

effect to these aims, the Land Reform (Scotland) Bill was introduced to the Scottish Parliament on 27 November 2001. Although there had been a prolonged prior consultation process, the Bill remained controversial and its legislative progress was slow. Royal Assent was received only on 25 February 2003, with full commencement expected during 2004.[1]

The Act is divided into three parts. Part 1 regulates the new access rights, or, as they have been described colloquially, the 'right to roam'. Part 2 establishes a right to buy in favour of rural community bodies. This is not an absolute right but is dependent on the current landowner deciding to sell, rather like a right of pre-emption. In contrast, Part 3, which introduces a right to buy in favour of crofting community bodies, is in absolute terms. The crofting community body, provided that it has fulfilled the relevant criteria, can exercise its right at any time.

Access rights

Section 1 of the Land Reform (Scotland) Act 2003 confers on the population at large certain 'access rights' to land. These are (1) the right to be, for specified purposes, on land, and (2) the right to cross land. These new rights are distinct from and do not affect existing access rights, for example a servitude or public right of way.[2] Certain activities are specifically excluded, in particular hunting, shooting and fishing, and using a motorised vehicle or vessel.[3] Thus the right to roam may not be exercised by car.

Specified purposes

The specified purposes in relation to (1) are set out in s 1(3) of the Land Reform (Scotland) Act 2003. There are three. The first is for 'recreational purposes'. This is not further defined, but the proposed Scottish Outdoor Access Code[4] (discussed below) gives examples under a number of headings: pastimes (eg watching wildlife, sightseeing and photography); family and social activities (eg short walks,[5] picnics and kite flying); active pursuits (eg canoeing, mountaineering, sailing and wild camping); and participation in events such as marathons and mountain biking competitions.

The second specified purpose for exercising access rights is 'carrying on a relevant educational activity', defined as relating to furthering the understanding of natural or cultural heritage.[6] This would include access by a leader and students to learn about wildlife or landscapes or geological features.[7]

---

1 At the time of writing, the only provisions in force are ss 8, 10 and 27. See the Land Reform (Scotland) Act 2003 (Commencement No 1) Order 2003, SSI 2003/427.
2 Land Reform (Scotland) Act 2003, s 5(3).
3 LR(S)A 2003, s 9.
4 Proposed Scottish Outdoor Access Code para 2.7. The Code is available from Scottish Natural Heritage's website: www.snh.gov.uk.
5 It might be wondered why long walks with one's family are not mentioned.
6 LR(S)A 2003, s 1(5).
7 Proposed Scottish Outdoor Access Code para 2.8.

The final purpose is 'carrying on, commercially or for profit, an activity which the person exercising the right could carry on otherwise than commercially or for profit.' This, rather unclear, provision would seem to authorise the activities of paid mountain guides and the like.

Excluded land

Access rights can be exercised above and below, as well as on, the surface of land,[1] with 'land' including bridges, inland waters, canals and the foreshore.[2] But the rights may not be exercised over the land listed in s 6 of the Land Reform (Scotland) Act 2003. The list is a long one and includes (1) buildings; (2) caravans, tents or other places providing people with privacy or shelter; (3) school grounds; (4) sports or other playing fields; (5) land to which access is prohibited by other legislation;[3] (6) land set out for a particular recreational purpose; (7) land on which building, civil engineering or demolition works are being carried out; and (8) land in which crops have been sown or are growing.[4] Three further types of land on the list require more detailed mention.

First, the access rights do not extend to 'sufficient adjacent land' to allow persons living in houses or the places mentioned in (2) above 'to have reasonable measures of privacy in that house or place to ensure that their enjoyment [thereof] is not unreasonably disturbed'.[5] The provision should protect the immediate vicinity of Skibo Castle and perhaps tempt Madonna back to Scotland, but its interpretation by the courts will be eagerly awaited. In the proposed Scottish Outdoor Access Code, Scottish Natural Heritage attempts to provide some guidance on the matter.[6] 'Sufficient adjacent land' is normally to mean an individual's garden. In relation to larger houses with what may be termed 'policies', the Code says that access rights do not apply to those parts 'intensively managed for the domestic enjoyment of the house'.

Examples given are lawns, flowerbeds, paths, seats, sheds, water features and summerhouses. 'Less intensively managed' parts, however, such as grasslands and woodlands, are to be subject to access rights. Despite this clarification, a strong element of subjectivity remains in relation to intensity of management. A fixed distance limitation might have been preferable.

Secondly, land open to the public in return for payment for at least 90 days in the year ending 31 January 2001, and which has continued since to be open on

---

1 Land Reform (Scotland) Act 2003, s 1(6).
2 LR(S)A 2003, s 32.
3 In this regard note the Land Reform (Scotland) Act 2003 (Directions for the Purposes of Defence or National Security) Order 2003, SI 2003/2250, made by the Secretary of State for Scotland under the Scotland Act 1998. This allows him to make directions excluding access rights for defence or national security reasons.
4 This may well include commercial woodland: see Alasdair G Fox 'Exercising rights on forestry access and limited partnerships' (2003) 48 *Journal of the Law Society of Scotland* Oct/53.
5 LR(S)A 2003, s 6(1)(b)(iv).
6 Proposed Scottish Outdoor Access Code paras 3.13–3.17.

payment, is not subject to access rights.[1] The date relates to when the draft Land Reform Bill was first published. It means that Blair Drummond Safari Park can continue to charge an admission fee, but, in principle, someone opening a new safari park (at least once the Land Reform (Scotland) Act 2003 is brought into force) cannot restrict access by fee-charging without taking some further step, such as asking the local authority for exemption.

Local authority exemptions form a third exclusion.[2] Any order by a local authority must be confirmed by the Scottish Ministers if it is to last for six or more days. Ministers also have powers to exempt land.[3]

Responsible conduct

Both the landowner and the person exercising access rights must act 'responsibly'.[4] The exercise of access rights is presumed to be responsible if does not 'cause unreasonable interference' to the rights of others, for example landowners or others taking advantage of their access rights.[5] Landowners are prohibited from taking any action which has 'the main purpose of preventing or deterring' the exercise of access rights.[6] This expressly includes putting up signs and fences.

The duty of care owed by landowners to individuals present on their land is unaltered by the Land Reform (Scotland) Act 2003.[7] Nevertheless, it is not unreasonable to suppose that more people may exercise access as a result of the legislation and that the risk of a civil action may increase. Owners may wish to take steps in relation to danger spots and to review their insurance cover.

Regulatory framework

Local authorities are given a wide-ranging regulatory role in relation to Part 1 of the Land Reform (Scotland) Act 2003. They can make byelaws, and install notices and fences as well as 'means of contributing to the comfort and convenience' of those exercising access rights.[8] Lavatories are expressly mentioned. Local authorities are also tasked with establishing a 'core path' plan, to facilitate public access.[9] The 2003 Act also imposes certain responsibilities on Scottish Natural Heritage, most notably the creation and issue of the Scottish Outdoor Access

---

1 Land Reform (Scotland) Act 2003, s 6(1)(f).
2 LR(S)A 2003, ss 6(1)(j), 11.
3 LR(S)A 2003, s 8.
4 LR(S)A 2003, ss 2, 3.
5 LR(S)A 2003, s 2(2).
6 LR(S)A 2003, s 14.
7 LR(S)A 2003, s 5(2).
8 LR(S)A 2003, ss 12, 15.
9 LR(S)A 2003, ss 17–22.

Code.[1] A draft was released in early 2003 with formal consultation ending on 30 June 2003. In January 2004 SNH published its proposed version, which it has submitted to Scottish Ministers for approval.[2] Before it comes into effect, the Code requires to be approved by resolution of the Scottish Parliament.[3] The Code contains much helpful detail about how access rights should be exercised. Its legal status, however, is not entirely clear.[4] The nearest equivalent is probably the Highway Code.

Rural community right to buy

The purpose behind Part 2 of the Land Reform (Scotland) Act 2003 is to empower communities in rural areas and enable them to take charge of their land. Examples of poor management by absentee landlords were cited by the Scottish Executive in justification, although the provisions remain controversial in some quarters.[5] The extent to which communities will take advantage of their new rights is unclear. On one view, most of the worst cases of absentee landlordism have already been addressed by community acquisitions. During the legislative process, the Rural Development Minister said that he did not believe that there would be a 'significant redistribution of land' but that the 2003 Act would 'redress the balance of landownership in Scotland'.[6] Time will tell.

Community bodies and applicable land

The Land Reform (Scotland) Act 2003 enables *community bodies* to apply to the Scottish Ministers for registration of a *community interest* in land. Registration is in a new register under the control of the Keeper, known as the *Register of Community Interests in Land*.[7] As well as ordinary land, an interest may be registered in respect of salmon fishings and mineral rights (although not minerals reserved to the Crown, nor coal).[8] Scottish Ministers will issue an order defining land over which an interest may not be registered – in practice land in

---

1 Land Reform (Scotland) Act 2003, s 10.
2 See www.snh.gov.uk.
3 LR(S)A 2003, s 10(5).
4 The Proposed Scottish Outdoor Access Code para 1.4 states: '[T]he Code is expected to be a reference point for determining whether a person has acted responsibly. For example, where a dispute cannot be resolved and is referred to the Sheriff for determination, the Sheriff will consider whether the guidance in the Code has been disregarded by any of the parties. In this sense, the Code may be said to have evidential status. Failure to comply with the Code, however, is not, of itself, an offence.'
5 For example, Bill Aitken MSP, the Conservative Party spokesman on the matter described it as 'a land-grab of which Robert Mugabe would have been proud.' See *Scottish Parliament Official Report* 23 January 2003 col 17377.
6 Justice 2 Committee, Stage 1 Report on the Land Reform (Scotland) Bill, para 75.
7 See A Ramage 'Keeper's Corner' (2003) 48 *Journal of the Law Society of Scotland* July/62.
8 LR(S)A 2003, s 33(6).

urban areas.[1] The first proposal was that settlements with a population greater than 3,000 would be excluded,[2] but the draft order published in August 2003 increases the threshold to 10,000.[3] Consultation on the draft order ended in November 2003 and the Executive's final decision is awaited. The order requires to contain or refer to a map, making it possible to ascertain where a settlement officially ends and the rural surrounds begin.[4]

A community body must be a company limited by guarantee, and its memorandum and articles require to include a definition of the community to which it relates, normally by postcode units.[5] In principle, there is no minimum or maximum number of units, but the body must normally have at least 20 members. The body also requires to satisfy Scottish Ministers that its main purpose is 'consistent with furthering the achievement of sustainable development'. This may preclude communities acquiring land for conservation.

Registration of community interests

Once formed, a community body applies to Scottish Ministers for registration of a community interest.[6] A separate application must be made in respect of each 'holding' of land, ie each parcel of land owned separately. When an application is made, there is a consultation exercise, with the views of the landowner, in particular, being taken into account. Whilst the application process is ongoing, the landowner and any creditor seeking to enforce a standard security are, in general terms, barred from dealing with the land. The prohibition is publicised in the Register of Community Interests in Land.

The criteria which Scottish Ministers must apply before approving registration of a community interest are set out in s 38 of the Land Reform (Scotland) Act 2003. There are five. First, the relevant land must be registrable land within the meaning of the 2003 Act. Secondly, a 'significant number' of the community members must have a 'substantial connection' with the land; or the land must be 'sufficiently near' to land in respect of which community members have a 'substantial connection' and the acquisition must be compatible with 'furthering the achievement of sustainable development'. The language here leaves a lot open to Ministerial discretion and may prove fertile ground for appeal. Thirdly, in the case of mineral rights and salmon fishings, the community must have a connection to adjoining land. This means either owning it or being in the process of acquiring it, or having registered or being in the process of registering a community interest in it. Fourthly, there must be a sufficient level of support

---

1 Land Reform (Scotland) Act 2003, s 33(3).
2 See Scottish Executive *Land Reform (Scotland) Bill Policy Memorandum* para 13.
3 See www.scotland.gov.uk/consultations/landreform/crtbcons.pdf. This would bring in an additional 117 settlements.
4 LR(S)A 2003, s 33(4).
5 LR(S)A 2003, s 34.
6 LR(S)A 2003, s 37.

within the community to justify the registration. In this regard, it is provided that Scottish Ministers *shall* regard approval of the application by 10% or more of community members as being a sufficient level of support, but approval by less than 10% *may* be regarded as sufficient. Finally, the registration of the community interest must be in the public interest. Scottish Ministers must make their decision within nine weeks of receipt of the application, and a statement of reasons must be given, along with details of appeals procedures.

Effect of registration: freezing of transfers

If the application is approved, the community interest will be entered into the Register of Community Interests in Land. The effect, in general terms, is to prevent the owner from transferring the land without first giving the community body an opportunity to purchase.[1] Likewise, the 'taking of any action with a view to transfer' is prohibited. Nonetheless, a number of transfers are exempt:[2]

(1)   transfers otherwise than for value;

(2)   most transfers in implement or pursuance of a court order;[3]

(3)   transfers between spouses who have separated;

(4)   transfers of croft land to crofters tenanting it;

(5)   transfers to statutory undertakers to enable them to carry on their under-taking (for example, widening a road);

(6)   transfers between companies in the same group;

(7)   transfers in terms of compulsory acquisition legislation;

(8)   transfers which vest land in insolvency officials; and

(9)   transfers following the assumption, resignation or death of partners or trustees.

Scottish Ministers may modify the list by statutory instrument.[4] Transfers in categories (1), (6) and (9) are barred if they form part of a scheme or arrangement designed to avoid the effect of the Land Reform (Scotland) Act 2003.[5]

A form of avoidance not struck at is the selling of a company rather than the land which it holds. Thus if Rural Co Ltd owns 1,000 hectares in respect of which Auchnashuggle Residents Ltd has registered a community interest, and Rural Co

---

1   Land Reform (Scotland) Act 2003, s 40.
2   LR(S)A 2003, s 40(4).
3   But not orders under the Conveyancing and Feudal Reform (Scotland) Act 1970, s 24 or decrees in actions of division and sale.
4   LR(S)A 2003, s 42.
5   LR(S)A 2003, s 43.

wants to sell to the Orinocan Offshore Trust, the trust could buy a majority share-holding in Rural Co and thus get round the 2003 Act. During the passage of the Bill, the Scottish National Party introduced an amendment to prevent such a scheme from working. Its spokesman[1] pointed out that a significant proportion of land in Scotland was owned by companies which have the sole purpose of holding land.[2] The amendment was incompetent because company law is reserved to Westminster, but the Minister indicated some willingness to monitor the situation for possible future action.[3]

Where land is the subject of an exempt transfer, a special clause must be entered into the disposition, most conveniently at the end. A deed without a clause will be rejected by the Keeper.[4] There are two types of clause. The first must be used in all exempt transfers. No statutory style is provided, but the clause must state which exempt provision applies so as to prevent section 40(1) (the general prohibition on transfer) from operating.[5] A suggested style for a gratuitous transfer is:

> And I certify that s 40(1) of the Land Reform (Scotland) Act 2003 does not apply to this transfer of land because it is a transfer within the meaning of s 40(4)(a) of that Act.

In addition, the second type of clause must also be used where the transaction might fall foul of the anti-avoidance provisions in the 2003 Act.[6] As was seen, three types of transfer potentially fall into this category: gratuitous transfers, transfers between companies in the same group, and certain transfers involving partners or trustees. The clause must state that the transfer does not form part of a scheme and is not one of a series of transfers designed to evade the 2003 Act. Again there is no statutory style, but the following is suggested:

> And I declare that this transfer of land does not form part of a scheme or arrangement and is not one of a series the main purpose or effect, or one of the main purposes or effects, of which is the avoidance of the requirements or the consequences of Part 2 of the said Act.[7]

A transfer which is not exempt is 'of no effect'.[8] The Keeper should reject the application for registration unless he is satisfied that the 2003 Act is not being breached, and if he does so there is an obligation to inform Scottish Ministers.[9] If

---

1 Mr Alasdair Morgan MSP.
2 *Scottish Parliament Official Report* 23 January 2003 col 17341.
3 *Scottish Parliament Official Report* 23 January 2003 col 17341 (Mr Allan Wilson MSP).
4 Land Registration (Scotland) Act 1979, s 4(5) (inserted by the Land Reform (Scotland) Act 2003, s 66).
5 LR(S)A 2003, s 43(2)(a).
6 LR(S)A 2003, s 43(2)(b).
7 It is possible to say 'said Act' because this clause will immediately follow the first special clause.
8 LR(S)A 2003, s 40(2). However, this is difficult to reconcile with the curative effect of the LR(S)A 1979, s 3(1)(a). Presumably title is conferred but the Register is inaccurate.
9 LR(S)A 1979, s 4(4) (inserted by the LR(S)A 2003, s 66).

a prohibited transfer is not noticed by the Keeper, the community body has ten years to challenge it.[1] A determination is then made by the Lands Tribunal. If it finds in favour of the community body, then the right to buy becomes immediately effectual.

A registered community interest lasts for five years,[2] comparable in effect to an inhibition. An application for renewal may be made within the last six months of the five-year period, but there is no fast-track procedure and the same process must be gone through as with the original application.

Exercise of right to buy

If the owner decides to sell while a community interest is current, he or she must inform the community body and Scottish Ministers.[3] The community body will be asked to confirm within 30 days that it wishes to exercise its right to buy. Assuming that it does, Scottish Ministers will arrange for the land to be valued at what amounts to market value.[4] If neither the owner nor the community body appeals against the valuation (to the Lands Tribunal), the community is then balloted on whether it wishes to proceed.[5] It will be taken to have approved the purchase if at least half of its members turn out to vote and a majority of those support the community body's plans. If, however, less than half vote, but a majority of those record their approval nonetheless, Scottish Ministers can only be satisfied that the community favours purchase if the proportion of those who did vote 'is, in the circumstances, sufficient to justify the community body's proceeding to buy the land'.[6]

Before finally approving the purchase, Scottish Ministers must have regard to criteria similar to those to be applied in deciding whether to register the community interest in the first place.[7] Assuming approval is given, the purchase will essentially proceed in the same way as an ordinary conveyancing transaction.

Effect on conveyancing practice

Once it is in force, Part 2 of the Land Reform (Scotland) Act 2003 will have some impact on ordinary conveyancing practice. Solicitors acting in the purchase of rural land may need to check the Register of Community Interests in Land for community interests, although, if the 2003 Act is not much used by communities, perhaps not in every case. The Law Society's Conveyancing Committee is currently considering how the profession should deal with the legislation. A cautious approach would be to add a clause to the standard offer, as follows:

---

1 Land Reform (Scotland) Act 2003, s 50.
2 LR(S)A 2003, s 44.
3 LR(S)A 2003, s 48.
4 LR(S)A 2003, s 59.
5 LR(S)A 2003, ss 51, 52.
6 LR(S)A 2003, s 51(2).
7 LR(S)A 2003, s 51(3).

Where all or part of the subjects are registrable land within the meaning of the Land Reform (Scotland) Act 2003, s 33, the seller will exhibit to the purchaser prior to the date of settlement a search in the Register of Community Interests in Land disclosing that as at the date of conclusion of missives there is no entry in the Register prohibiting the seller from transferring the subjects to the purchaser.

No later search will be required, nor is there any need for the letter of obligation to be altered, because an application for registration of a community interest after missives are concluded must be turned down by Scottish Ministers.[1] It remains to be seen whether a clause on the above lines will become standard practice, or whether the purchasers will simply rely on the seller's general obligation to provide a good and marketable title.

Crofting community right to buy

The crofting community right to buy is not a right of pre-emption but is exercisable at any time. This difference apart, Part 3 of the Land Reform (Scotland) Act 2003 follows closely the scheme for the rural community right to buy set out in Part 2 and described above.[2] It is, of course, more limited in that it only applies in the six crofting counties of Argyll, Caithness, Inverness, Orkney and Shetland, Ross and Cromarty, and Sutherland. A crofting community body, like a rural community body, must be a company limited by guarantee and there are similar requirements as regards its memorandum and articles.[3]

The land which may be purchased is essentially crofting land, within the meaning of the Crofters (Scotland) Act 1993, along with common grazings.[4] The right extends to salmon fishings in waters within or beside the croft land, but only if the crofting community body is simultaneously purchasing the land to which the fishings relate, or it has purchased that land within the last year.[5] The body is also entitled to purchase what the 2003 Act calls 'eligible additional land', which means land contiguous to the croft land being purchased and owned by the same party.[6] Likewise, it can purchase 'eligible sporting interests' which means rights under contract or lease to shoot or fish on the land.

Where the crofting community body wishes to purchase eligible additional land and the owner does not consent, the matter must be referred to the Land

---

1 Land Reform (Scotland) Act 2003, s 39(5).
2 At the time of writing, the Scottish Executive was engaged in a consultation process in relation to the regulations setting out the form of application and other matters in relation to Part 3. The consultation period ended on 9 March 2004. See www.scotland.gov.uk/consultations/rural/ croftright.pdf.
3 LR(S)A 2003, s 71.
4 LR(S)A 2003, s 68.
5 LR(S)A 2003, s 69. Similarly, mineral rights may be purchased if related croft land is being simultaneously purchased or was purchased within the last five years.
6 LR(S)A 2003, s 70.

Court.[1] Conversely, the owner of eligible additional land *not* included within the crofting community body's original application may ask Scottish Ministers to require that the crofting community body modify the application to include that land.[2] Before doing so, Scottish Ministers must be satisfied that this in the public interest. Section 83 facilitates the leaseback of any sporting interests to the landowner once the crofting community body has acquired the land.

As with Part 2, there are procedures for valuing the land, assessed at the date when Scottish Ministers consented to the application.[3] Appeals against valuation are to the Land Court.[4] The Crofters Commission is required to set up a Register of Crofting Community Rights to Buy.[5]

Stamp duty land tax[6]

The basic law

For conveyancing transactions, stamp duty land tax (SDLT) replaced stamp duty on 1 December 2003.[7] The legislative framework is set out in Part 4 of the Finance Act 2003 (as supplemented, and in some cases amended, by regulations).[8]

SDLT is a tax on *land transactions* and not, as with stamp duty, on instruments.[9] A 'land transaction' is 'any *acquisition* of a *chargeable interest*',[10] and a 'chargeable interest' is:[11]

(1)   an estate, interest, right or power in or over land in the United Kingdom, or

(2)   the benefit of an obligation, restriction or condition affecting the value of any such estate, interest, right or power,

other than an exempt interest.

'Acquisition' has an extended meaning under s 43 of the Finance Act 2003:

---

1 Land Reform (Scotland) Act 2003, s 77.
2 LR(S)A 2003, s 79.
3 LR(S)A 2003, s 88.
4 LR(S)A 2003, s 92.
5 LR(S)A 2003, s 94.
6 This part is contributed by Alan Barr of the University of Edinburgh.
7 For transitional arrangements, see the Finance Act 2003, Sch 19.
8 Notably the Stamp Duty and Stamp Duty Land Tax (Variation of the Finance Act 2003) (No 2) Regulations 2003, SI 2003/2816; the Stamp Duty Land Tax (Consequential Amendment of Enactments) Regulations 2003, SI 2003/2867; the Stamp Duty and Stamp Duty Land Tax (Consequential Amendment of Enactments) Regulations 2003, SI 2003/2868; the Stamp Duty Land Tax (Amendment of Schedule 5 to the Finance Act 2003) Regulations 2003, SI 2003/2914; and the Stamp Duty Land Tax (Amendment of Schedule 4 to the Finance Act 2003) Regulations 2003, SI 2003/3293.
9 FA 2003, s 42(2).
10 FA 2003, s 43(1).
11 FA 2003, s 48(1).

(3) For the purposes of this Part –

    (a) the creation of a chargeable interest is –

        (i) an acquisition by the person becoming entitled to the interest created and

        (ii) a disposal by the person whose interest or right is subject to the interest created;

    (b) the surrender or release of a chargeable interest is –

        (i) an acquisition of that person by any person whose interest or right is benefited or enlarged by the transaction, and

        (ii) a disposal by the person ceasing to be entitled to that interest; and

    (c) the variation of a chargeable interest is –

        (i) an acquisition of a chargeable interest by the person benefiting from the variation, and

        (ii) a disposal of a chargeable interest by the person whose interest is subject to or limited by the variation.

As a result, a whole range of land transactions is caught by the new tax, and a surprisingly large number of transactions which involve rights in both directions will be treated as (at least) two land transactions. The tax applies however the acquisition is effected – whether by act of the parties, by order of a court or other authority, or by operation of law.

Generally, the effective date of a transaction, from which payment and reporting obligations will derive, is 'completion' (ie settlement).[1] But where a land transaction involves both a contract and a conveyance, and the contract is substantially performed ahead of completion, the substantial performance becomes the effective date of the transaction.[2] 'Substantial performance' takes place where the 'purchaser'[3] takes possession of the whole, or substantially the whole, of the subject matter of the contract, or a substantial amount of the consideration is paid. In the case of a lease, this means the first payment of rent. Otherwise it usually means payment of 90% of the total consideration. The completion, if and when it occurs, is also a notifiable transaction, but tax paid on the earlier substantial performance can be set off against that due on completion. If the contract is later annulled, the tax is repaid.

The creation of an option or right of pre-emption (as opposed to but in addition to its later exercise) is itself a land transaction.[4] Where, therefore, a pre-emption is reserved in a sale, the seller is a 'purchaser' with respect to the land transaction

---

1 Finance Act 2003, ss 119, 121.
2 FA 2003, s 44.
3 Defined widely in FA 2003, s 43(4) to include any person acquiring the subject matter of the transaction, such as a lessee.
4 FA 2003, s 46.

constituted by the pre-emption. Similarly, an excambion involves two distinct land transactions.[1]

The purchaser is liable for payment of SDLT and, as with stamp duty, registration in any register maintained by the Keeper of the Registers of Scotland requires evidence of compliance.[2]

Rates of tax

SDLT is charged as a percentage of the *chargeable consideration* for a transaction, rounded down to the nearest whole pound.[3] Usually the chargeable consideration is simply the price, but a number of special rules are set out in Schedule 4 to the Finance Act 2003. VAT is included unless it can only be charged by virtue of an election to waive exemption after the effective date of a transaction. Except in the case of leases, discussed below, the rates are:

Rate %	Ordinary land		Land in disadvantaged areas	
	Residential	Non-residential	Residential	Non-residential
0	Up to £60,000	Up to £150,000	Up to £150,000	All
1	Over £60,000–250,000	Over £150,000–250,000	Over £150,000–250,000	
3	Over £250,000–500,000	Over £250,000–500,000	Over £250,000–500,000	
4	Over £500,000	Over £500,000	Over £500,000	

'Residential property' means a building that is used, or suitable for use, as a dwelling, and includes the grounds of such a building.[4] But where six or more dwellings are the subject of a single transaction they lose their status as residential. 'Disadvantaged areas' are, in Scotland, defined by postcode.[5]

Transactions which are 'linked' are viewed as a single transaction, with SDLT payable at the rate applicable to the total consideration.[6] Transactions are considered as linked if they form part of a single scheme, arrangement or series of transactions between the same vendor and purchaser or persons connected with them (such as spouses, siblings, or the corporate equivalent).[7] The inclusion of connected persons extends the 'series of transactions' rule familiar from stamp duty. So if a house is sold to a man and the garden to his wife, the two transactions would usually be treated as linked.

---

1 Finance Act 2003, s 47.
2 FA 2003, ss 79, 85(1). As for evidence of compliance, see p 000.
3 FA 2003, s 55.
4 FA 2003, s 116. Subsections (2) and (3) provide firm classifications for some borderline cases, such as halls of residence.
5 For a complete list, see *Conveyancing 2001* pp 41–3. See generally the FA 2003, Sch 6, and the Stamp Duty (Disadvantaged Areas) Regulations 2001, SI 2001/3747, which are applied in relation to stamp duty land tax by Sch 6, para 2.
6 FA 2003, s 55(4).
7 FA 2003, s 108, applying the definition of connected persons in the Income and Corporation Taxes Act 1988, s 839.

Leases

Rates

As with stamp duty, leases receive separate treatment. A distinction is made between *rent* and *premiums* (or other capital payments).

Premiums are treated in the same way as consideration for other land transactions (already discussed), except that the 0% rate is raised to 1% if the annual rent exceeds £600. Among the exclusions from chargeable consideration are reverse premiums and the renunciation of an existing lease.[1]

Rent is taxed on the basis of *net present value* ('NPV'), as follows:[2]

Rate %	Ordinary land		Land in disadvantaged areas	
	Residential	Non-residential	Residential	Non-residential
0	Up to £60,000	Up to £150,000	Up to £150,000	All
1	Over £60,000	Over £150,000	Over £150,000	

Unlike the usual rule for SDLT, the 1% rate is only paid on the balance above the threshold limits. These rates are alleged to remove 60% of commercial leases and 90% of residential leases from the charge to SDLT, although the percentages (especially the first) are hotly disputed.

Net present value

The NPV is the total rent payable over the term of the lease, but discounted at the rate of 3.5% a year to reflect the fact that future rent payments are of less value than payments made at present. Subject to an anti-avoidance provision, increases in rent more than five years into a lease (whether by rent review or otherwise) are ignored. Increases within the first five years are the subject of an initial estimate which is then adjusted, at the end of the five-year period, by taking the rent for the rest of the lease to be the highest amount paid in any previous period of 12 months. This rule applies also to turnover rent, ie rents based on the tenant's turnover.

Amendments are promised to aid calculation of the length of a lease for the purposes of NPV. Break and forfeiture clauses and options to renew are to be disregarded. And while extensions during the term of a lease, including extensions by tacit relocation, are to be treated as new leases, they are linked transactions and, hence, notifiable if the total duration exceeds seven years. As a result, leases extended by tacit relocation are much more likely to suffer SDLT than a new lease for a year, which would not necessarily be a linked transaction with any previous lease.

---

1 Finance Act 2003, Sch 4, paras 14, 15.
2 See generally FA 2003, Sch 5.

Completion

'Completion' – the date in relation to which reporting and payment obligations arise – is, for Scotland, the date on which the lease is signed by the parties (or presumably the last date if more than one), or is constituted by any means. Difficulties remain. For instance, what happens when entry is given on the basis of an agreement for lease, with draft attached, but no formal lease is executed?

Exemptions and reliefs

As with all taxes, much revolves around what is provided by way of exemptions and reliefs. The following are among the more important:

(1) any security interest;[1]

(2) a licence to use and occupy land.[2] Arrangements which qualify as a licence in England and Wales are, however, often classified as a lease in Scotland;

(3) no chargeable consideration – typically outright gifts.[3] This important exemption sweeps up various things that used to require self-certification under the Stamp Duty (Exempt Instruments) Regulations 1987,[4] for example transfers to and from trusts in many cases and distributions from executries;

(4) certain transactions involving land in disadvantaged areas – as already mentioned;[5]

(5) certain purchases and grants of lease of dwellings by registered social landlords;[6]

(6) certain transactions in connection with divorce;[7] and

(7) purchases by charities.[8]

Notification and certificates

Introduction

Perhaps the single greatest change from stamp duty lies in the administrative and notification requirements. The completion of an SDLT return is required in many cases where there is no tax to be paid – most notably where there

---

1 Finance Act 2003, s 48(2)(a).
2 FA 2003, s 48(2)(b).
3 FA 2003, Sch 3, para 1.
4 Stamp Duty (Exempt Instruments) Regulations 1987, SI 1987/516.
5 FA 2003, Sch 6.
6 FA 2003, s 71, Sch 3, para 2.
7 FA 2003, Sch 3, para 3.
8 FA 2003, s 68, Sch 8. There are anti-avoidance provisions.

is consideration but this falls below the zero percentage threshold. In addition, many transactions in which the tax is wholly relieved also require a return.

The basic rule is that a *land transaction return* must be delivered to the Revenue within 30 days in respect of every *notifiable transaction*.[1] Failure to do so attracts an initial penalty of £100, which rises in cases of further delay.[2] In practice, most returns will be made well within 30 days in order to allow registration. But problems can easily be imagined. For instance, it may not be appreciated that a return may be required in a case where no action was needed under stamp duty rules and no SDLT is actually payable. Further, the time limit applies to the return as a whole. Thus an incomplete return may fail to fulfil the obligation, with possibly unpleasant consequences.

Notifiable transactions

There are three categories of notifiable transactions.[3] The first is the grant of a lease, either for seven years or longer (whether or not tax is payable) or for less than seven years (but only where tax is payable). The second is the acquisition of a *major interest in land* – defined to mean ownership or the tenant's interest in a lease.[4] So dispositions of land or assignations of leases are notifiable under this heading. The third is the acquisition of any other interest in land (such as real burdens or servitudes) if SDLT is chargeable or would be chargeable but for a relief. The threshold of £60,000 for SDLT means that in practice few transactions in this category will be notifiable.

Land transaction returns

A land transaction return must be in the prescribed form, contain the prescribed information, and include a declaration by the purchaser that the return is to the best of his or her knowledge correct and complete.[5] The basic return (SDLT 1) is a six-page form, with pay-slip attached. Further details are required on supplementary forms in certain cases. An SDLT 2 is required where there are more than two sellers and/or purchasers, and an SDLT 3 where land requires a detailed description so that it can be identified in the absence of a normal postal address. Complex commercial transactions use SDLT 4, but these include any transaction in which a new lease is involved and/or the purchaser is a company.

In general, the return must actually be signed by the purchaser, and if there is more than one, all must sign. But an attorney acting under a power of attorney

---

1 Finance Act 2003, s 76(1).
2 FA 2003, Sch 10, paras 3, 4.
3 FA 2003, s 77.
4 FA 2003, s 117(3).
5 FA 2003, Sch 10, para 1(1).

can sign instead provided the capacity is indicated in the form. For companies the return is completed by the secretary or 'another person for the time being having the express, implied or apparent authority to act on its behalf for the purpose'.[1] In the case of trustees, any trustee can make the return.[2] It is not clear whether this applies to partners acting as trustees for a partnership – especially as the guidelines indicate that if more than four partners are acting as trustees, only the first four should sign the declaration on the return. By a separate provision, partnerships can act through a representative partner nominated by a majority of the partners,[3] but this may not apply to land held by trustees for the partnership.

In the case of a chargeable transaction, the return must include an assessment of the tax due and be accompanied by payment;[4] but sometimes no tax will be due. When the form has been completed correctly, submitted to the data capture centre in Netherton, and payment has been made, the Revenue issues a *certificate* (SDLT 5) confirming compliance with SDLT requirements.

If, later, a purchaser finds that information on the return was incorrect, he or she must inform the Revenue without unreasonable delay. Otherwise a penalty is due.[5] Records must be kept for six years after the transaction.[6]

Self-certificates

It is only on production of the certificate or of a *self-certificate* that a document will be accepted by the Keeper for registration in any register maintained by him.[7] Hence, if the transaction does not need to be notified, a self-certificate is used, to the effect that no land transaction return is required.[8] This will be the case, for instance, for grants of rights other than ownership and lease where, as in almost every case, the consideration is less than £60,000. It will also be the case for a number of short leases, and possibly for other transactions where it is desired to record documents in the Books of Council and Session.

Immediate registration: personal presentation in Edinburgh

Of course there can be circumstances where immediate registration is required. Provision has been made for this, after long negotiation, and the following statement agreed:[9]

---

1 Finance Act 2003, s 100(2).
2 FA 2003, Sch 16, para 6(1).
3 FA 2003, Sch 15, para 8.
4 FA 2003, s 76(3).
5 FA 2003, Sch 10, para 8.
6 FA 2003, Sch 10, para 9.
7 FA 2003, s 79(1).
8 FA 2003, s 79(3)(b). The regime for penalties, record-keeping and inquiries is set out in Sch 11.
9 Between the Law Society of Scotland and the Inland Revenue.

In Scotland, a purchaser (or tenant under a lease of more than 20 years) obtains no property rights in the land at all until such time as his or her title is registered in the Land Register. There is thus a gap between completion and registration, during which period purchasers in Scotland face the risk of losing the property if, despite the purchaser having paid the price, the sellers become insolvent prior to the purchasers' title being registered or if fraudulent sellers re-convey to a third party acting in good faith (but who has been duped by the seller) before registration of the first purchaser's title.

In many transactions, the risk to the purchaser is addressed in part by the issue of letters of obligation by the seller's solicitors. In some cases, for example when purchasing from a receiver, no letters of obligation are granted. In other cases, for example where the seller is a company, letters of obligation are granted but on behalf of the client. In such cases, the purchaser may wish to register immediately and could be prejudiced by the delay inherent in submitting a return and receiving a certificate in each case by post. Special arrangements have been made to permit personal presentation of the SDLT returns in Edinburgh in these cases.

The solicitor wishing to present personally can sign a declaration setting out why the 'same day' service is required. This should be presented in person together with the completed form SDLT 1 (and any supplementary returns required) and payment (or evidence thereof) to the Edinburgh Stamp Office within two working days of the effective date of the transaction. Assuming that the returns are in order, the Edinburgh Stamp Office will give the solicitor a handwritten SDLT certificate. The date on which the land transaction return was presented to the Edinburgh Stamp Office will count as the date on which the transaction was notified to the Inland Revenue.

The SDLT certificate can then be taken to the Registers with the documents so that registration can take place. The Edinburgh Stamp Office will send the land transaction return(s) to Netherton and they will be processed in the usual manner.

When can the special arrangements be used? The intention is not to replace the usual process for all transactions in Scotland. Assuming that the new system works as planned, it should be possible for a certificate to be received by the purchaser's solicitors well within the usual 21-day period of letters of obligation. The special arrangements are intended to focus on transactions where there is a real risk to the purchaser if the transaction is not registered on the day of settlement or the next day. The special arrangements are intended to apply to transactions where there are no letters of obligation or, as in the case where the seller is a company, where letters of obligation are granted but only on behalf of the client.

Therefore the special arrangements for personal presentation will be available for:

(1) any transaction where the seller is a corporate entity and the seller's solicitor has not given a solicitor's personal letter of obligation in respect of the charges register and the company file;

(2) any other transaction where the seller's solicitor has been requested to give a solicitor's personal letter of obligation but has refused to do so; and

(3) any transaction where the purchaser needs to register ownership on or before obtaining access to the transaction funding.

In all cases, the special arrangements can only be used if the SDLT returns are presented to the Edinburgh Stamp Office within two working days of the effective date of the transaction.

It should be noted that the special arrangements can also be used for the grant of a lease where the landlord is a corporate entity, provided that registration is required to give the tenant a real right.

The fact that no SDLT is payable due to the availability of a relief such as group relief will not prevent the special arrangements from being available.

Other administrative provisions

The legislation contains a vast amount of regulatory provisions on the administration of stamp duty land tax, mostly imported directly from other tax regimes. There are rules on the duty to keep and preserve records; on the power of the Revenue to make inquiries and to make determinations where no return is delivered; on the power to the Revenue to make assessments; in relation to appeals against Revenue decisions on tax; and on many other things. The basic legislative code[1] has now been followed by further administrative provisions in the Stamp Duty Land Tax (Administration) Regulations 2003, SI 2003/2837.

Solicitors should be aware that a person who assists in the preparation of information to be used for the purposes of tax and which is known to be incorrect is liable to a penalty not exceeding £3,000.[2] Furthermore, conviction under this provision entitles the Revenue to require the delivery of any tax-related documents in respect of any (other) client.[3]

---

1 Contained, principally, in the Finance Act 2003, Schs 10–14.
2 FA 2003, s 96.
3 FA 2003, Sch 13, para 14. The person in question must have 'stood in relation to others as a tax accountant' but this is widely defined.

Part V

Part V: Tables

Cumulative table of appeals 2003

This lists all cases digested in *Conveyancing 1999* and subsequent annual volumes in respect of which an appeal was subsequently heard, and gives the result of the appeal.

Anderson v Express Investment Co Ltd
2002 GWD 28-977, OH (2002 Case (5)) *affd* 11 Dec 2003, IH (2003 Case (13))

Armstrong v G Dunlop & Sons' Judicial Factor
2004 SLT 155, OH (2002 Case (48)) *affd* 2003 GWD 31-858, IH (2003 Case (39))

Burnett's Trustee v Grainger
2000 SLT (Sh Ct) 116 (2000 Case (21)) *rev* 2002 SLT 699, IH (2002 Case (19)) *affd* 2004 GWD 9-211, HL

Caledonian Heritable Ltd v Canyon Investments Ltd
2001 GWD 1-62, OH (2000 Case (69)) *rev* 2002 GWD 5-149, IH (2002 Case (61))

Cheltenham & Gloucester plc v Sun Alliance and London Insurance plc
2001 SLT 347, OH (2000 Case (63)) *rev* 2001 SLT 1151, IH (2001 Case (73))

Conway v Glasgow City Council
1999 SCLR 248, 1999 Hous LR 20, Sh Ct *rev* 1999 SLT (Sh Ct) 102, 1999 SCLR 1058, 1999 Hous LR 67 (1999 Case (44)) *rev* 2001 SLT 1472, 2001 SCLR 546, IH (2001 Case (51))

Glasgow City Council v Caststop Ltd
2002 SLT 47, OH (2001 Case (6)) *affd* 2003 SLT 526, IH (2003 Case (6))

Grampian Joint Police Board v Pearson
2000 SLT 90, OH (2000 Case (18)) *affd* 2001 SC 772, 2001 SLT 734, IH (2001 Case (17))

Inverness Seafield Co Ltd v Mackintosh
1999 GWD 31-1497, OH (1999 Case (19)) *rev* 2001 SC 406, 2001 SLT 118, IH (2000 Case (13))

Kaur v Singh (No 2)
1999 Hous LR 76, 2000 SCLR 187, 2000 SLT 1324, OH (1999 Case (34)) *affd* 2000 SLT 1323, 2000 SCLR 944, IH (2000 Case (26))

Labinski Ltd v BP Oil Development Co
2002 GWD 1-46, OH (2001 Case (16)) *affd* 2003 GWD 4-93, IH (2003 Case (17))

McAllister v Queens Cross Housing Association Ltd
2001 Hous LR 143, 2002 SLT (Lands Tr) 13 (2002 Case (26)) *affd* 2003 SC 514, 2003 SLT 971, IH (2003 Case (28)).

Minevco Ltd v Barratt Southern Ltd
1999 GWD 5-266, OH (1999 Case (41)) *affd* 2000 SLT 790, IH (2000 Case (36))

Robertson v Fife Council
2000 SLT 1226, OH (2000 Case (84)) *affd* 2001 SLT 708, IH (2001 Case (82)) *rev* 2002 SC (HL) 145, 2002 SLT 951, 2002 Hous LR 78, 2003 SCLR 39 (2002 Case (69))

Royal Bank of Scotland plc v Wilson
2001 SLT (Sh Ct) 2 (2000 Case (53)) *affd* 2003 SC 544, 2003 SLT 910, 2003 SCLR 716, IH (2003 Case (40))

Scottish Youth Theatre (Property) Ltd v RSAMD Endowment Trust Trustees
2002 SCLR 945, OH (2002 Case (3)) *affd* 2003 GWD 27-758, IH (2003 Case (8))

Souter v Kennedy
(23 July 1999, unreported), Perth Sheriff Court (1999 Case (69)) *rev* (20 March 2001, unreported), IH (2001 Case (81))

Spence v W & R Murray (Alford) Ltd
2001 GWD 7-265 (Sh Ct) (2001 Case (9)) *affd* 2002 SLT 918, IH (2002 Case (1))

Stevenson v Roy
2002 SLT 445, OH (2002 Case (67)) *affd* 2003 SC 544, 2003 SCLR 616, IH (2002 Case (54))

Tesco Stores Ltd v Keeper of the Registers of Scotland
2001 SLT (Lands Tr) 23 (2001 Case (30)) *affd* sv *Safeway Stores plc v Tesco Stores Ltd* 2003 GWD 20-610, IH (2003 Case (25))

Thomas v Allan
2002 GWD 12-368 (Sh Ct) (2002 Case (7)) *affd* 2004 GWD 1-15, IH (2003 Case (22))

Wilson v Inverclyde Council
2001 GWD 3-129, OH (2001 Case (29)) *affd* 2003 SC 366, 2004 SLT 265, IH (2003 Case (27))

Table of cases digested in earlier volumes but reported in 2003

A number of cases which were digested in *Conveyancing 2002* or earlier volumes but were at that time unreported have been reported in 2003. A number of other cases have been reported in an additional series of reports. For the convenience of those using earlier volumes all the cases in question are listed below, together with a complete list of citations.

Armstrong v G Dunlop & Sons' Judicial Factor
2004 SLT 155

Balfour (Earl of), Petitioner
2002 SLT 1385, 2003 SC (HL) 1, 2003 SCLR 125

Bank of Ireland v Morton
2003 SC 258

Broadway v Clydesdale Bank plc
2003 SLT 707

Glasgow City Council v Morrison Developments Ltd
2003 SLT 263, 2003 SCLR 276

MacAlister v Wallace
2003 SCLR 773

Robertson v Fife Council
2002 SC (HL) 145, 2002 SLT 951, 2002 Hous LR 78, 2003 SCLR 39

Sheltered Housing Management Ltd v Cairns
2003 SLT 578, 2002 Hous LR 126